Steck Vaughn

WONDERS OF SCIENCE

Teacher's Edition

Plant Life

Joan S. Gottlieb

C O N T E N T S

**Meet your state standards with free blackline masters and links to other materials at
www.HarcourtAchieve.com/AchievementZone.**
Click Steck-Vaughn Standards.

Harcourt Achieve

Rigby • Steck-Vaughn

www.HarcourtAchieve.com
1.800.531.5015

Wonders of Science Program

❏ The Earth and Beyond

❏ The Human Body

❏ Land Animals

❏ Matter, Motion, and Machines

■ Plant Life

❏ Water Life

About the Author

Joan S. Gottlieb taught at the elementary and secondary levels for more than ten years. She received a Ph.D. in education from the University of South Carolina. Dr. Gottlieb holds B.A., B.S., and M.Ed. degrees from the University of Minnesota.

ISBN 0-7398-9186-3

© 2004 Harcourt Achieve Inc.

Rigby and Steck-Vaughn are trademarks of Harcourt Achieve Inc. registered in the United States of America and/or other jurisdictions.

1 2 3 4 5 6 7 8 862 11 10 09 08 07 06 05 04

Scope and Sequence

	UNIT 1	UNIT 2	UNIT 3	UNIT 4	UNIT 5	UNIT 6	UNIT 7	UNIT 8
The Human Body	How the Body Is Organized	Body Systems	More Body Systems	The Nervous System	Human Reproduction	Diseases	Avoiding Health Problems	First Aid
Land Animals	Animal Adaptations	Invertebrate Animals	Amphibians	Reptiles	Birds	Mammals	Conservation	
Plant Life	Plants Are Living Things *Communicating Observing Making Models*	Flowers *Communicating Observing Interpreting Data*	Grasses and Cereals *Communicating Classifying Interpreting Data*	Trees *Communicating Classifying Observing*	Plants Used as Food *Communicating Classifying Inferring*	Plant Adaptations *Communicating Classifying Making Models*	Plant Products *Communicating Making Models Inferring*	Conservation *Communicating Observing Inferring*
Water Life	Water Environments	Water Plants	Invertebrate Water Animals	Fish	Water Reptiles	Water Birds	Water Mammals	Conservation
The Earth and Beyond	The Solar System	Weather	Land and Water	Regions of Earth	Shaping the Surface	The Changing Earth	Materials of Earth	Conservation
Matter, Motion, and Machines	Matter	Changes in Matter	Nature's Energies	Sound and Light	Magnetism and Electricity	Motion and Forces	Machines	Technology

About the Program

Wonders of Science was developed for students with special needs, including students in special education programs, students receiving remedial instruction, and students in regular classes who read at a second-to-third-grade reading level. This six-book program presents current science topics in a simple, straightforward manner.

Wonders of Science was written by a classroom teacher who has faced the difficulties of teaching junior and senior high school special-needs students without suitable teaching materials. Like most teachers of special-needs classes, she invested uncountable hours preparing materials that would capture her students' interest and offer them a chance to succeed.

Wonders of Science is a result of field testing a variety of activities in classes with a wide range of reading abilities, intellectual capacities, ages, maturity levels, social backgrounds, interests, attention spans, and physical capabilities. The end result is a program designed to appeal to a wide variety of special-needs students. This program offers a structured curriculum, yet it helps students develop the much needed skill of working independently.

Features of the Program

❏ All lessons are complete on one or two pages. Brief reading selections provide students with successful experiences. Students with short attention spans are not frustrated by lesson length.

❏ Scientific vocabulary appears in boldfaced type. Each vocabulary word is also defined in the Glossary at the back of the book.

❏ In the Teacher's Edition, words that may be unfamiliar or difficult for students are underlined. These words may need further explanation.

❏ Assessment in the form of exercises is included in every lesson to check retention of important scientific concepts. Unit and Mastery Tests are also provided.

❏ A one-page review at the end of each unit helps prepare students for the unit test. Student performance on the review can be used to plan reteaching activities based on individual needs before students take the unit test.

❏ *Explore & Discover,* a self-directed, hands-on activity at the end of each unit, provides students with an opportunity to develop process skills and reinforce concepts taught in the unit. These activities call for easy-to-obtain and use materials. Students should be more comfortable with familiar materials than with expensive scientific hardware and apparatus. Yet the physical and cognitive skills used are the same.

❏ In each unit test, main ideas and scientific concepts are presented in a format that incorporates standardized test items as well as open-ended sections.

❏ Teaching Strategies for each lesson are provided in the Teacher's Edition. These strategies, in the form of activities, provide support, reinforcement, and extension of concepts through real-life application, hands-on activities, or discussion.

❏ A *Just for Fun* page for each unit is included in the Teacher's Edition. This blackline master presents key scientific concepts from the unit in a puzzle format and can be used as reinforcement.

❏ Special Projects in the Teacher's Edition are motivational activities that supplement and provide enrichment to each unit. Read through the projects before beginning a unit to determine when each is most helpful to your class.

❏ A two-part Mastery Test is included in the Teacher's Edition for assessing student comprehension of key concepts. The Mastery Test is written in the same format as the unit tests to ease test anxiety and promote student success.

Meet your state standards with free blackline masters and links to other materials at **www.HarcourtAchieve.com/AchievementZone**. Click **Steck-Vaughn Standards**.

Using the Program

The *Wonders of Science* program was designed to be used flexibly. You are encouraged to use the materials in a way that best meets the needs of your students. For example, you may wish to introduce the vocabulary words first, and then have students read each lesson independently. Or, for students who are able to work independently, you may encourage use of the Glossary as an aid for defining new scientific vocabulary.

All exercise directions are shown in color and are, therefore, easily distinguished. Each exercise format is repeated throughout the text so that students become familiar with the directions.

The design of each page is friendly and easy to use. All text is contained in a box to help students focus on the lesson. A color band runs down the side of the reading passage to cue the student on what to read. Directions are set in color to cue the student when a new activity starts. Photographs and art are used to reinforce and illustrate scientific concepts.

Correlation to
Benchmarks for Science Literacy

In an effort to guide reform in science, mathematics, and technology education, the American Association for the Advancement of Science published the report *Benchmarks for Science Literacy* in 1993. This report specifies how students should progress toward science literacy, recommending what they should know and be able to do by the time they reach certain grade levels. Intended as a tool for designing curriculum, *Benchmarks* describes levels of understanding and ability for *all* students. Steck-Vaughn's *Wonders of Science* provides special-needs students with opportunities to build the common core of learning recommended by *Benchmarks*. In *Plant Life,* students can also explore their individual interests and abilities by examining topics such as tropical rain forests, special adaptations of plants, and products made from plants.

***Wonders of Science: Plant Life* will be useful in helping students attain the following specific science literacy goals set out in *Benchmarks*:**

Chapter 1: THE NATURE OF SCIENCE
Section C: The Scientific Enterprise
Important contributions to the advancement of science, mathematics, and technology have been made by different kinds of people, in different cultures, at different times.

Section C: The Scientific Enterprise
No matter who does science and mathematics or invents things, or when or where they do it, the knowledge and technology that result can eventually become available to everyone in the world.

Chapter 3: THE NATURE OF TECHNOLOGY
Section A: Technology and Science
Technology is essential to science for such purposes as access to outer space and other remote locations, sample collection and treatment, measurement, data collection and storage, computation, and communication of information.

Section C: Issues in Technology
The human ability to shape the future comes from a capacity for generating knowledge and developing new technologies—and for communicating ideas to others.

Chapter 5: THE LIVING ENVIRONMENT
Section A: Diversity of Life
One of the most general distinctions among organisms is between plants, which use sunlight to make their own food, and animals, which consume energy-rich foods. Some kinds of organisms, many of them microscopic, cannot be neatly classified as either plants or animals.

Section A: Diversity of Life
Animals and plants have a great variety of body plans and internal structures that contribute to their being able to make or find food and reproduce.

Section A: Diversity of Life
All organisms, including the human species, are part of and depend on two main interconnected global food webs. One includes microscopic ocean plants, the animals that feed on them, and finally the animals that feed on those animals. The other web includes land plants, the animals that feed on them, and so forth. The cycles continue indefinitely because organisms decompose after death to return food material to the environment.

Section B: Heredity
In some kinds of organisms, all the genes come from a single parent, whereas in organisms that have sexes, typically half of the genes come from each parent.

Section D: Interdependence of Life
In all environments—freshwater, marine, forest, desert, grassland, mountain, and others—organisms with similar needs may compete with one another for resources, including food, space, water, air, and shelter. In any particular environment, the growth and survival of organisms depend on the physical conditions.

Section D: Interdependence of Life
Two types of organisms may interact with one another in several ways: They may be in a producer/consumer, predator/prey, or parasite/host relationship. Or one organism may scavenge or decompose another. Relationships may be competitive or mutually beneficial. Some species have become so adapted to each other that neither could survive without the other.

Section E: Flow of Matter and Energy
Food provides the fuel and the building material for all organisms. Plants use the energy from light to make sugars from carbon dioxide and water. This food can be used immediately or stored for later use. Organisms that eat plants break down the plant structures to produce the materials and energy they need to survive. Then they are consumed by other organisms.

Section F: Evolution of Life
Small differences between parents and offspring can accumulate (through selective breeding) in successive generations so that descendants are very different from their ancestors.

Section F: Evolution of Life
Individual organisms with certain traits are more likely than others to survive and have offspring. Changes in environmental conditions can affect the survival of individual organisms and entire species.

Chapter 12: HABITS OF MIND
Section D: Communication Skills
Organize information in simple tables and graphs and identify relationships they reveal.

Section D: Communication Skills
Read simple tables and graphs produced by others and describe in words what they show.

Section D: Communication Skills
Locate information in reference books, back issues of newspapers and magazines, compact disks, and computer databases.

Master Materials List
Explore & Discover Activities

The following list is designed to help you acquire and keep track of materials for the **Explore & Discover** activities in this book. These materials are commonly available in classrooms, or may be purchased at supermarkets or discount stores, or brought from students' homes.

The quantities and groupings may be adjusted depending on the needs of your class, and in some cases you may want to substitute materials. The page numbers of the activities are provided to help your planning.

	Item	Quantity	Notes
Unit 1 **Plants Are** **Living Things** *page 22*	paper, poster	1 sheet per student	Also used in Unit 8
	scissors	1 pair per student	Also used in Unit 5
	magazines (to cut up)	several per class	Also used in Unit 5
	markers	1 per student	Also used in Units 5, 8
	glue	several bottles per class	Also used in Unit 5
	encyclopedia or gardening guide	1 or more per class	Also used in Units 4, 5
Unit 2 **Flowers** *page 38*	seeds, packages	2 per student	
	containers, milk carton or yogurt	2 per student	
	potting soil	enough to fill containers	
	dishes, plant	2 per student	
	paper, graph	1 sheet per student	
Unit 3 **Grasses and** **Cereals** *page 54*	labels, nutrition facts from cereal box	1 per student	
	paper, unlined, large	1 sheet per student	
Unit 4 **Trees** *page 78*	paper, drawing	1 sheet per student	Also used in Units 5, 6
	paper, lined, writing	1 sheet per student	
	paper, tracing	1 sheet per student	
	tape measures	several per class	
	crayons	1 per student	
	encyclopedia or tree guide	1 or more per class	Also used in Units 1, 5
Unit 5 **Plants Used** **as Food** *page 96*	paper, butcher	1 sheet per class	
	markers	1 set per class	Also used in Units 1, 8
	magazines (to cut up)	several per class	Also used in Unit 1
	paper, drawing	1 sheet per student	Also used in Units 4, 6
	scissors	1 pair per student	Also used in Unit 1
	glue	several bottles per class	Also used in Unit 1
	index cards	1 per student	
	encyclopedia or food guide	1 or more per class	Also used in Units 1, 4
Unit 6 **Plant Adaptations** *page 112*	plants, dandelion	1 per student	
	plants, local	1 or more per student	
	paper, drawing	1 sheet per student	Also used in Units 4, 5
	plant field guide	1 or more per class	
Unit 7 **Plant Products** *page 124*	containers, 1/2 gallon	1 per pair	
	water	enough to fill containers	
	newspaper	1 sheet per pair	
	screen, 10" x 10" aluminum	several per class	
	eggbeaters	several per class	
	trays, cafeteria	several per class	
	boards, 1" x 10"	several per class	
Unit 8 **Conservation** *page 136*	boxes, large, sturdy	several per class	
	newspapers (for recycling)	any amount	
	paper, poster	1 sheet per student	Also used in Unit 1
	markers	several sets per class	Also used in Units 1, 5

UNIT 1 — Plants Are Living Things

Unit 1 explains what plants are and describes their main parts. The unit discusses the ability of plants to make food and explores the ways in which plants reproduce. It describes several ways plants can be grouped. It also describes organisms that have some plantlike characteristics. Finally, the unit distinguishes between plants without tubes, such as mosses and algae, and plants with tubes, such as ferns and seed plants.

Page 4—What Is a Plant?

Help students summarize what they have learned about plants. Make a list of plant characteristics on the chalkboard:

- ❏ made of cells
- ❏ can grow
- ❏ can make their own food
- ❏ have ways to reproduce
- ❏ cannot move from place to place

Then ask students how plants are different from animals. They should indicate that animals can move around on their own but cannot make their own food. Finally, tell students that animals are like plants in some ways. Animals are made of cells. They can grow and they have ways to reproduce.

Page 6—Parts of a Plant

Materials: common house plant, radish seeds, paper towel, two saucers, magnifying glass

Display a common house plant in the classroom. Point out the stem of the plant and the leaves. Ask students what function the root of the plant has. (It holds the plant in the soil. It takes in water and minerals from the soil.) Germinate some radish seeds so that students can see a root and root hairs. Soak a paper towel with water. Place it in a saucer. Put several radish seeds on the towel and cover with another dish. After a few days, the radish seeds should have begun to sprout. Have students examine the root with a magnifying glass to see the tiny root hairs.

Page 8—Plants Make Food

Materials: leafy green house plant, such as a geranium; petroleum jelly, aluminum foil

Show students that plants cannot make their own food without certain substances. Place a healthy house plant in a sunny location. Coat two leaves top and bottom with petroleum jelly. Cover two other leaves completely with aluminum foil. Keep the plant watered. After three days, have the students examine the leaves. The untreated leaves should be green and healthy. Both the jelly-coated leaves and those covered with foil should be yellow and weak. The jelly prevents carbon dioxide from entering the leaves. Without this gas, the leaves cannot make food. The foil prevents sunlight from reaching the leaves. Photosynthesis cannot take place without the sun.

Page 10—How Plants Reproduce

Materials: seeds, small clay pots, sand, soil, labels, marking pens

Bring in a variety of seeds. Have students compare them and note any differences they observe. Students may want to plant some of the seeds and care for the growing plants. Put sand or soil in small clay pots. Have students select one type of seed for each pot and push several seeds below the surface of the soil. Then students should label each pot with the type of seed planted. Water the pots when the soil becomes dry. When seedlings begin to grow, put the pots in a sunny location.

Page 12—How Plants Are Grouped

Help students understand that it is possible to group the same things in several ways. For example, ask students how they would group the objects in the classroom. They may suggest grouping by color, by size, by material, or by how the objects are used.

Page 14—Fungi

Point out to students that many living things belong to the fungi group. All fungi are alike in some ways. They can grow and reproduce. But without chlorophyll they cannot make their own food. Fungi are both helpful and harmful. Some students may have heard of the athlete's foot fungus that grows on human skin and causes it to become red, flaky, and itchy. But remind students that other fungi are helpful because they decompose dead plant and animal matter, making soil richer.

Page 15—Molds

Materials: slice of white bread, plastic sandwich bag and twist tie, magnifying glass

Expose a slice of white bread to the air for several minutes. Mold spores in the air will land on the bread. Then moisten the bread slightly and place it in a plastic sandwich bag. Close the bag tightly with a twist tie. After several days mold should have grown on the bread.

Allow students to look at the mold through the bag with a magnifying glass. (**Caution:** *Do not open the bag. Some students may be allergic to molds. Dispose of the bag properly after the class is over.*) Tell students that the mold has tiny rootlike parts that grow into the bread. These parts digest the food material of the bread and absorb it.

Page 16—Yeasts
Materials: package of dried yeast, microscope, slides, cover slips, glass, spoon, medicine dropper, sugar, warm water

Stir a teaspoon of sugar into a glass of warm water. Add dried yeast and let the mixture stand for a day. Place a drop of the mixture on a microscope slide and cover with a cover slip. Have the students look at the slide under low and high power. Help them locate individual yeast cells and any cells that are budding. Remind students that yeasts reproduce by forming buds.

Page 17—Mushrooms
Materials: several large mushrooms (from a grocery store), white paper

Students may be able to see the spores of a mushroom. Remove the stalks from several large mushrooms. Place the caps on a sheet of white paper. After a day, lift the caps off the paper. Spores from the caps should be visible. Remind students that mushrooms reproduce from spores.

Page 18—Algae
Point out that there are many kinds of algae. Some are one-celled, while others can grow to be 30 yards long. Algae are food for many water animals. Also, as they make food, algae release oxygen into the water. Both water and land animals take in this oxygen as they breathe. Algae are also used as food, as fertilizers, and as thickeners in salad dressings and ice cream.

Page 19—Mosses
Materials: moss plants, magnifying glass

Moss plants may be found growing in damp areas or on the trunks of trees. If possible collect some moss plants and bring them to class for the students to examine. Use a magnifying glass to help the students see the tiny leaves. Some moss plants may have cases where the spores are formed. Have students look for small, round structures growing at the tops of thin stalks.

Page 20—Ferns and Seed Plants
Materials: fresh celery stalk, red food coloring, glass, water, knife

Put a celery stalk in a glass of water that has been colored a dark red with food coloring. Let the celery stand overnight. Then have the students look at the stalk. The coloring will allow them to see the tubes in the stalk.

Page 22—Plant Parts We Eat
This activity reinforces the process skill *Making Models* as students identify foods from plants and categorize them by the part of the plant eaten. Tally and chart responses to the question at the end of the activity to see which part of a plant the entire class eats most often.

UNIT 2   Flowers

Unit 2 describes the parts of a flower. It explains how pollination takes place, producing seeds for the reproduction of the plant. The unit describes how seeds are dispersed. Finally, it describes different kinds of flowers and defines perennials, annuals, and wildflowers.

Page 24—The Parts of a Flower
Materials: several large flowers (tulip, lily, gladiolus), razor blade, magnifying glass, tweezers

Point out the sepals and the petals as students examine a whole flower. Using tweezers, remove these parts carefully. Point out the stamens and the pistil. Review with students the function of each of these parts. Let students examine the parts with a magnifying glass. Next, point out the ovary. Carefully cut open the ovary with a razor blade. Using the magnifying glass, have students examine the ovules inside.

Page 26—Pollination
To help students summarize what they have learned about pollination, start a webbing diagram on the chalkboard. The diagram might look like this:

Then ask volunteers to add other elements from the lesson, such as pollen, stamen, pistil, nectar, bees, butterflies, moths, and bats.

Page 28—How Seeds Travel
Materials: encyclopedia

Interested students may want to research other types of seeds that "travel." Suggest that they investigate milkweed, thistle, tumbleweed, coconut, or the cottonwood tree.

Page 30—Daisies

Materials: plant catalog, seed packages, or field guide

Have students look through a plant catalog, seed packages, or a field guide to see varieties of daisies. Students may learn what colors daisies can be, how long they take to grow from seeds, and where they grow.

Page 31—Tulips

Let students know that tulips were brought to Europe from Turkey in the 1500s. The name *tulip* comes from the Turkish word for *turban*. By the seventeenth century, tulips had become so popular that people would pay huge amounts of money for a bulb.

Page 32—Violets

Materials: encyclopedia, plant catalog, or field guide

Inform students that pansies are flowers related to violets. Have students find out more about pansies. Ask them to research how many petals pansies have, what colors the flowers are, and whether they are perennials.

Page 33—Wildflowers

Materials: field guide or encyclopedia

Students may be interested to know about the wildflowers that grow in their region. Encourage them to consult an encyclopedia or a field guide to find out about these flowers.

Page 34—Orchids

Tell students that many people grow orchids as a hobby. You may want to invite a local florist to speak to the class. The florist can explain what conditions are needed to grow different kinds of orchids, how long it takes for the plants to grow from seeds, and what types can be grown at home.

Page 36—Asters

Materials: asters, magnifying glass

Have students examine the ray flowers and disk flowers of an aster. Pull out a ray flower (a petal) and a disk flower (a tube in the middle of the flower). Let students look at each and find all the other parts of the flower.

Page 38—Grow Your Own Garden

This activity engages students in the process skill *Observing* as they watch their seedlings emerge and grow into young plants. Allow students to help select the seeds to grow. Students may enjoy growing herbs or flowers that can later be transplanted into an outdoor garden.

UNIT 3   Grasses and Cereals

Unit 3 describes grass plants and cereal grasses. The concept of annual and perennial plants is reviewed. Lawn grasses, sugarcane, and bamboo are provided as examples of grasses. The cereal grasses described are wheat, corn, rice, and oats. The importance of these plants is discussed.

Page 40—Grasses

Help students summarize what they have learned about grasses. Start a webbing diagram on the board. Your diagram might look like this:

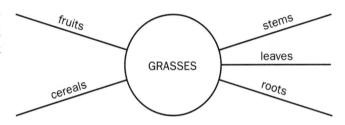

Then ask volunteers to add details from the lesson to the diagram.

Page 42—Lawn Grasses and Weeds

If possible visit a nearby gardening center. Find out what kinds of grasses grow well in your area. Students may have questions, such as which weeds harm each kind of grass, how to get rid of the weeds, and under what conditions do the grasses grow best.

Page 44—Wheat

Ask students to look at labels of foods in their home or in the grocery store to find products that contain wheat. They should then make a list of these items and bring their lists to class. Make a master list of all the items.

Page 46—Corn

Materials: encyclopedia, poster paper, marking pens

Have students make a bulletin board display that shows all the ways in which corn is used. They should include food for animals, different ways people eat corn, and products, such as dyes, fuels, fertilizers, paints, and so on. They may want to consult an encyclopedia for other products.

Page 48—Rice

If possible ask the school dietitian to speak to the class about the differences between brown rice and white rice. Have students be prepared with a short list of questions.

Page 50—Oats
Materials: labels from several kinds of cereals containing oats

Have students examine the list of ingredients from several boxes of oat cereal. Point out that the ingredient present in the greatest amount is listed first. Are oats always listed first? Do all the cereals have sugar added? Are chemicals added to all the cereals? Help students decide which cereal has the fewest additives.

Page 51—Sugar Cane
Let students know that sugar cane is only one source of sugar. Sugar is also obtained from the root of the sugar beet. Russia is the largest producer of sugar beets. In the United States, sugar beets grow in California, Colorado, Michigan, and other states.

Page 52—Bamboo
Students may be interested to learn about the giant panda. These animals live in China and feed mainly on bamboo shoots. About every 100 years, all the bamboo plants produce seeds and then die. The last time this took place was in the late 1970s. This left the panda without a food supply for several years until the seeds grew into new plants. During that time about one fourth of the giant pandas died. Giant pandas are now protected by law.

Page 54—Compare the Nutrition of Cereal Grains
Students will gain experience in the process skill *Interpreting Data* as they compare the nutritional values of various breakfast cereals. Provide several extra Nutrition Facts labels for students to complete their charts. Students will discover that wheat and oat cereals have the highest protein and fiber content. It is also interesting to compare the sugar content of various cereals.

UNIT 4 Trees

Unit 4 describes the largest green plants—trees. The unit identifies the parts of a tree and describes how a tree grows. It distinguishes between deciduous and evergreen trees and discusses three different types of forest environments. Finally, the unit describes specific kinds of trees, including maples, oaks, palms, sequoias, and magnolias.

Page 56—The Parts of a Tree
On the chalkboard, reproduce the drawing of the tree from the lesson. Ask volunteers to label each part. Review with students what the function of each part is. Finally, ask students how trees are like other green plants. (They have roots, stems, and leaves. The leaves make food.)

Page 58—How a Tree Grows
Materials: samples of growth rings (from a biological supply house or lumber yard)

Show students a sample of a set of growth rings. Help them identify thick rings and thin rings. Thick rings form in years when there is a lot of rain, while thin rings form in years when there is little rain.

Page 60—Evergreen Trees
Materials: cones and needles from different evergreen trees, field guide

Have students look at a variety of needles and cones from different evergreen trees. Use a field guide to identify the kind of tree each came from.

Page 62—Deciduous Trees
Materials: poster paper, marking pens, field guide

Have students make a bulletin board display showing a deciduous tree in all four seasons. Use a field guide to help students select a tree and to provide details about the shape of the leaves, the flowers, the kind of bark, and so on. Label the drawings with the name of the tree and the season.

Page 64—Deciduous Forests
Materials: encyclopedia

Have students research deciduous forests in an encyclopedia. Ask them to find a map that shows the parts of North America where deciduous forests are found. Help them find out if your state is within this region.

Page 66—Coniferous Forests

Emphasize to students that the lesson describes two kinds of coniferous forests. One kind of forest grows in cold climates and the other grows in a warm, wet climate. The trees that grow in these forests are different, too. Spruce, fir, and pines grow in a cold climate, while giant sequoias and redwoods grow in a warm climate.

Page 68—Tropical Rain Forests

Materials: encyclopedia (or atlas)

Show students a world map where forest areas are indicated. Point out the regions where tropical rain forests grow. Show students the area surrounding the Amazon River in South America. Tell students that in one square mile of forest there may be as many as 100 different kinds of trees.

Page 70—Maple Trees

Ask students to write a short paragraph on maple trees. They should use their own words to describe what they remember about the trees from the lesson. To help them compose their paragraphs, put these main points on the chalkboard:

- ❑ deciduous
- ❑ broad, flat leaves
- ❑ seeds like wings
- ❑ how people use maple trees

Page 71—Oak Trees

Help students distinguish between deciduous oaks and evergreen oaks. Put these two lists on the chalkboard:

Deciduous
- ❑ grow where winters are cold
- ❑ leaves change with the seasons

Evergreen
- ❑ grow where weather is warm most of the year
- ❑ stay green all year

Finally, ask students how deciduous oaks and evergreen oaks are alike. (They live for hundreds of years. They grow from acorns.)

Page 72—Palm Trees

Materials: encyclopedia, poster paper, marking pens

Have students make a bulletin board display showing different kinds of palm trees. They can use the information from the lesson, supplemented by an encyclopedia article if necessary. They should draw two kinds of palm trees, one with fan-shaped leaves and another with feather-shaped leaves. They should label each drawing and indicate what products, if any, come from each tree.

Page 74—Sequoia Trees

Materials: encyclopedia

Divide the class into four groups. Ask each group to research one of the following: the sequoias, the General Sherman Tree, Sequoia National Park, and the Cherokee named "Sequoya." (Sequoya invented a system of writing for the Cherokee people. The sequoia tree is named after him.) Ask a representative from each group to present a report on their topic to the class.

Page 76—Magnolia Trees

Let students know that the tree in the photograph, a southern magnolia, can grow to a height of about 100 feet. Its leaves are about 8 inches long and are green and shiny on top and rusty on the underside. Large, white flowers bloom in early summer.

Page 78—Adopt a Tree

In this activity students adopt a nearby tree while exploring the process skill *Observing*. Encourage students to learn more about their adopted tree or your own state's tree from library books or an encyclopedia. Invite students to plan an Arbor Day celebration at your school on April 28.

Mastery Test, Part A, covering units 1–4 can be found on page T15.

UNIT 5   Plants Used as Food

Unit 5 explores the ways in which people use different parts of plants as food. These parts include leaves, roots, stems, seeds, bulbs and tubers, flowers, and fruits. The unit discusses specific foods in each group and lists some of the nutrients each food provides.

Page 80—Food from Green Plants

Materials: nuts, brown paper bag

Ask students why plants are an important part of a healthy diet. (They make carbohydrates, fats, proteins, and vitamins.) Remind students why they need the substances plants make. (The body gets energy from carbohydrates and fats. It uses proteins to grow and repair tissue. Vitamins help the other substances to work.)

Test for fat in foods. Rub a nut on a brown paper bag. The nut, which contains fat, leaves a shiny spot on the paper. The students may want to try this with other foods, such as potatoes, bacon, butter, and a green vegetable.

Page 81—Leaves

Tell students that vitamin C and vitamin K are found in both spinach and cabbage. Vitamin C helps to keep teeth healthy and helps wounds to heal. Vitamin K helps in the process of normal blood clotting. Let students know that even very small amounts of vitamins are needed by the body.

Page 82—Roots

Materials: carrots or radishes (with their tops)

Some students may not be aware that carrots and radishes are the roots of plants. If possible show students a carrot or radish with the green leaves still attached. Review the concept of vitamins. Remind students that vitamins are found naturally in foods, not just in supplements, and that a healthy diet should include all the vitamins a person needs.

Page 84—Stems

Remind students of what they learned about sugarcane in Unit 3. Sugarcane is a perennial grass. Its stems are ground up and made into sugar. Sugar is a carbohydrate and provides energy. Fiber is also a carbohydrate, but it is not broken down in the body. Some sources of fiber are stems, such as celery and rhubarb, carrots, skins of fruits and vegetables, and grains, such as wheat, corn, and oats.

Page 86—Seeds

Materials: a seed package of kidney beans or lima beans, magnifying glass

Students can see the tiny plant inside a seed. Soak bean seeds in water overnight. Carefully remove the seed coat and separate the seed leaves. Using a magnifying glass, help students see the tiny plant, or embryo, attached to one of the seed leaves. The seed leaves store food for the embryo until it can make food on its own.

Page 88—Bulbs and Tubers

Materials: onion, garlic bulb, potato with eyes

Help students distinguish between roots and tubers. Roots are the parts of plants that take in water and minerals from the soil. Tubers are enlarged underground stems. (Students may remember from Unit 3 that some grasses have underground stems from which new grass plants grow.) Both roots and tubers can store food made by a plant. Bulbs grow underground, too. They are thick, fleshy leaves wrapped around a stem.

You may want to cut open an onion to show students the leaves where the food is stored. Also, pull apart a garlic bulb so students can see the separate cloves. If possible show students a potato with "eyes." Each eye can grow into a new potato plant.

Page 90—Flowers

Materials: stalk of broccoli and cauliflower, whole cloves, glass, water, knife

Cut a stalk of cauliflower down the middle. Students should be able to see the small, tight buds at the top of the thick, fleshy stalk.

Place a stalk of fresh broccoli in a glass of water. After a few days, the buds will open and small yellow flowers will be visible.

Show students some cloves. Remind them that cloves are the buds of the flowers of clove trees.

Page 92—Fruits

Materials: seeds from oranges, grapefruit, or cherries; small clay pot, soil

Have students save seeds from oranges, grapefruit, or cherries used at home. They can plant the seeds in soil in a small clay pot. When plants get larger, they can be transplanted into a larger pot. Plants should be kept in a sunny location.

Page 94—Growing Vegetables

If any of the students (or their parents) grow vegetables, ask them to speak to the class about their gardens. Other students should prepare a list of questions to ask the speaker.

Page 96—Create a Salad Collage

This activity reinforces the process skill *Classifying* as students make a collage of plants used in salads and create their own recipes for a class cookbook. Help students generate an extensive list of ingredients by giving clues for less common foods, such as olives, spinach, chickpeas, or kiwi fruit.

UNIT 6 Plant Adaptations

Unit 6 defines *environment* and *adaptation*. It explains that plants in different environments have different adaptations. Specific adaptations, such as parasitism, poison, and spines, are mentioned with an explanation of how each helps a plant survive.

Page 98—How Adaptations Help Plants

Remind students that plants living in different environments need different adaptations to survive. After they read about the ocotillo, ask if they think this plant would grow in a tropical rain forest where there may be more than 100 inches of rain in a year. Help students realize that the ocotillo has adaptations for a desert environment. Plants of the tropical rain forest do not need adaptations that help them get and store water, since water is so abundant.

Page 100—Parasitic Plants

Tell students about the Indian paint brush plant, which is common in the western United States, especially in mountain elevations. Indian paint brush is either wholly or partially parasitic. It has a pretty flower, but it gets nourishment from the roots of other plants. Ask students to speculate about using Indian paint brush in a garden.

Page 102—Plants That Attract Insects

Students should understand that pollination takes place when pollen from the stamen is transferred to the pistil. Pollination can take place within a flower or between two flowers of the same type. After pollination takes place, the flower begins to make seeds. Also remind students that bees and other insects get food from flowers. They feed on pollen and on nectar made inside the flowers.

Page 104—Poisonous Plants

Help students learn to identify plants, such as poison ivy, poison oak, and poison sumac, that produce an unpleasant rash when they come in contact with the skin. Students should also learn that tasting any unknown plant or its fruit or berries, or any fungi is dangerous. If a scouting manual is available, consult it to learn about wild plants. Students should never eat wild plants without first consulting an adult.

Page 106—Plants with Spines

Materials: encyclopedia or books on desert plants, poster paper, marking pens

Have students research the large variety of plants that grow in a desert environment. Encourage them to make a display showing many of these plants.

Page 108—Insect-Eating Plants

Tell students about the sundew, an insect-eating plant. Each leaf is covered with hairs that release a sticky liquid. When an insect gets caught in the hairs, the plant digests the trapped insect.

Page 110—The Ant and the Acacia Tree

Tell students about a relationship between a plant and an animal in which both benefit. The yucca is a plant that grows in Central America. It is pollinated by one kind of moth. In turn, the yucca seeds are food for the caterpillars that hatch from the moth's eggs. The yucca could not form seeds without the moth, and the caterpillars could not develop without the yucca.

Page 112—Find Plant Adaptations

This activity reinforces the process skill *Classifying* as students find examples of plant adaptations in plants growing nearby. Indoor plants can also be used for this activity. Review plant adaptations with students and discuss how your area's climate (temperature, wind, precipitation) may affect plant adaptations that students observe.

UNIT 7 Plant Products

Unit 7 describes a range of products obtained from plants. The processes are explained, and the importance of a variety of plants is emphasized. These products include wood, paper, medicines, cloth, and rubber.

Page 114—Wood

Challenge your students to name as many things as they can that are made of wood. Write each item on the chalkboard. Besides the items mentioned in the lesson, students may think of fences, baseball bats, toys, broom handles, boxes, signs, barrels, and so on. Help students realize that trees are cut down for the wood to make these products. New trees can be planted, but it takes many years for them to grow.

Page 116—Paper

Materials: encyclopedia

Have students research the history of paper. They can learn about the invention of paper. They can also find out how the use of paper spread. Ask students to find out how paper was first made in the U.S. or Canada.

Page 118—Medicines

Remind students that penicillin is made from a mold, a plantlike organism. (You may want to review the characteristics of mold.) In 1928 Alexander Fleming, a British scientist, discovered that penicillin growing in a laboratory dish killed the bacteria around it. Penicillin has been used to treat many serious infections caused by bacteria.

Page 120—Cloth

Materials: spinach or collard greens, pot, heat source, glass bowl, small piece of white cotton or wool fabric, water

Tell students that parts of plants can be used to make dyes for cloth. Help students make natural dye by boiling plant parts. Remove the plant parts and let the dye cool before pouring it in a glass bowl. Add the fabric to be dyed and let it sit until the desired color is reached. Encourage students to find out about dyes from plants. The Navajo, for example, use many kinds of plants to dye the wool they use to make rugs. Students can research this topic in the encyclopedia or in a book on Native Americans.

Page 122—Rubber

Start a webbing diagram on the chalkboard. Write the word *RUBBER* within a circle. On lines radiating from the circle, write words that describe the properties of rubber: elastic, long-lasting, waterproof, does not let electricity pass through. Have volunteers write in products that demonstrate each property.

Page 124—Make Your Own Recycled Paper

This activity gives students insight as to how paper products are made while engaging in the process skill *Making Models*. A blender or food processor can be used with adult supervision to improve the pulp-making process. Be sure to use plenty of water when blending to prevent strain on the motor.

UNIT 8   Conservation

Unit 8 describes the different factors that constitute a threat to plants. It distinguishes between endangered and extinct plants. Finally, it presents some positive ways in which people can help protect plants.

Page 126—Protecting Plants

Explain to students that plants and animals are renewable resources. But if they are destroyed faster than they can reproduce, they may become endangered. Plants provide oxygen that people and other animals breathe, they are a source of food, and they provide many useful products.

Page 128—Endangered Plants

Remind students that tropical rain forests have the greatest variety of plants and animals. Scientists believe there are plants in the rain forests that have not yet been discovered. When the forests are destroyed, both the plants and the animals die out because the animals need the plants in order to live.

Page 130—Forest Conservation

Materials: encyclopedia

Have students use an encyclopedia to find a national forest in their area or nearby. Encourage students who have visited a national forest to tell the class about their experience.

Page 132—Forests in Danger

Materials: map of the United States

The destruction of the rain forest affects more than just the places where the forests are located. Have a volunteer read the last paragraph of the lesson aloud. Ask students to look at a map of the United States and try to determine what cities could be affected if coastlines were flooded.

Page 134—People Can Protect Plants

Students can help protect plants. They can be careful not to disturb areas where wildflowers are growing. They can visit national forests and learn more about endangered plants.

Page 136—Start a Recycling Program

This activity implements the process skill *Communicating* as students organize a newspaper recycling program.

Mastery Test, Part B, covering units 5–8 can be found on page T17.

Mastery Test

Fill in the circle in front of the word or phrase that best completes each sentence. The first one is done for you.

1. All plants are made of
   - (a) fungi.
   - (b) spores.
   - ● cells.

2. Roots, stems, and leaves are the main parts of
   - (a) animals.
   - (b) plants.
   - (c) fungi.

3. The way plants make food is called
   - (a) photosynthesis.
   - (b) reproducing.
   - (c) budding.

4. Moving pollen from a stamen to a pistil is called
   - (a) pollination.
   - (b) photosynthesis.
   - (c) exchange.

5. Pollen is made in the top part of the
   - (a) pistils.
   - (b) stamens.
   - (c) petals.

6. Insects that come to flowers feed on
   - (a) petals.
   - (b) ovules.
   - (c) nectar.

7. The most important crop in the United States is
   - (a) corn.
   - (b) rice.
   - (c) lawn grass.

8. Tree roots that branch out are called
   - (a) fibrous roots.
   - (b) taproots.
   - (c) trunks.

9. Grass stems that grow underground are called
   - (a) joints.
   - (b) leaves.
   - (c) rhizomes.

10. Food for a tree is made in the
    - (a) roots.
    - (b) stems.
    - (c) leaves.

Mastery Test

Use the words below to complete the sentences.

annual	food	stem
deciduous	roots	

11. Green plants are living things that can make their own

    _____.

12. The _____ of a tree take in water and minerals from the soil.

13. A _____ tree rests in winter.

14. Sugar is made from the _____ of sugar cane.

15. _____ grasses die at the end of the growing season.

Write the word or words that best finish each sentence.

16. In the ovary of a flower, male cells from the pollen tube join with egg cells,

    or _____.

17. Flowers with bright colors and nice smells are usually pollinated by

    _____.

18. Chlorophyll in a plant's leaves takes in energy from the

    _____.

19. Magnolia trees are evergreens in the southern United States and are

    _____ in the North.

Write the answer on the lines.

20. Explain why photosynthesis is important.

    _____

    _____

Mastery Test

Fill in the circle in front of the word or phrase that best completes each sentence. The first one is done for you.

1. One green leafy vegetable is
   - ⓐ beans.
   - ⓑ broccoli.
   - ● cabbage.

2. Seeds and fruits are formed by
   - ⓐ bulbs.
   - ⓑ flowers.
   - ⓒ leaves.

3. Places where plants and animals live are called
   - ⓐ environments.
   - ⓑ adaptations.
   - ⓒ deserts.

4. The natural fiber used most in the United States comes from
   - ⓐ rubber trees.
   - ⓑ cotton plants.
   - ⓒ oak trees.

5. Insects are attracted to
   - ⓐ tall plants.
   - ⓑ colorful flowers.
   - ⓒ green leaves.

6. Most paper is made from
   - ⓐ cloth.
   - ⓑ plastic.
   - ⓒ wood.

7. Spines are an adaptation of
   - ⓐ cactus plants.
   - ⓑ poison ivy.
   - ⓒ mushrooms.

8. A plant becomes extinct when every one of its kind has
   - ⓐ moved away.
   - ⓑ died.
   - ⓒ started to grow.

9. An endangered plant is so rare it can only be found growing in
   - ⓐ small numbers.
   - ⓑ large numbers.
   - ⓒ cold areas.

10. Today, much of the rain forest is being
    - ⓐ cut down and burned.
    - ⓑ planted with new trees.
    - ⓒ blown away by the wind.

Mastery Test

Fill in the missing words.

11. The plant that a parasitic plant lives on is called a _____.
    (host, acacia)

12. People eat the parts of plants where _____ stored.
    (flowers are, food is)

13. Wood is the part of a tree that forms under the _____.
    (leaves, bark)

14. Water, soil, and _____ are natural resources.
    (plastic, minerals)

Use the words below to complete the sentences.

cellophane	elastic	water
chemicals	stem	

15. Because rubber is _____, it can stretch and go back to its original shape.

16. Water is stored in the _____ and branches of a cactus.

17. Wood pulp is used to make a thin, clear material called _____.

18. To grow vegetables, you need good soil, plenty of _____, and the right amount of sunlight.

19. Certain _____ that get into the air and water can harm plants and animals.

Write the answer on the lines.

20. Name the parts of the plant that hold the seeds.

    _____

    _____

    _____

Mastery Test

Fill in the circle in front of the word or phrase that best completes each sentence. The first one is done for you.

1. All plants are made of
   - ⓐ fungi.
   - ⓑ spores.
   - ● cells.

2. Roots, stems, and leaves are the main parts of
   - ⓐ animals.
   - ⓑ plants.
   - ⓒ fungi.

3. The way plants make food is called
   - ⓐ photosynthesis.
   - ⓑ reproducing.
   - ⓒ budding.

4. Moving pollen from a stamen to a pistil is called
   - ⓐ pollination.
   - ⓑ photosynthesis.
   - ⓒ exchange.

5. Pollen is made in the top part of the
   - ⓐ pistils.
   - ⓑ stamens.
   - ⓒ petals.

6. Insects that come to flowers feed on
   - ⓐ petals.
   - ⓑ ovules.
   - ⓒ nectar.

7. The most important crop in the United States is
   - ⓐ corn.
   - ⓑ rice.
   - ⓒ lawn grass.

8. Tree roots that branch out are called
   - ⓐ fibrous roots.
   - ⓑ taproots.
   - ⓒ trunks.

9. Grass stems that grow underground are called
   - ⓐ joints.
   - ⓑ leaves.
   - ⓒ rhizomes.

10. Food for a tree is made in the
   - ⓐ roots.
   - ⓑ stems.
   - ⓒ leaves.

T15

Mastery Test

Use the words below to complete the sentences.

annual	food	stem
deciduous	roots	

11. Green plants are living things that can make their own **food**.

12. The **roots** of a tree take in water and minerals from the soil.

13. A **deciduous** tree rests in winter.

14. Sugar is made from the **stem** of sugar cane.

15. **Annual** grasses die at the end of the growing season.

Write the word or words that best finish each sentence.

16. In the ovary of a flower, male cells from the pollen tube join with egg cells, or **ovules**.

17. Flowers with bright colors and nice smells are usually pollinated by **insects**.

18. Chlorophyll in a plant's leaves takes in energy from the **sun**.

19. Magnolia trees are evergreens in the southern United States and are **deciduous** in the North.

Write the answer on the lines.

20. Explain why photosynthesis is important.
    Photosynthesis is the way that plants make food.

T16

Mastery Test

Fill in the circle in front of the word or phrase that best completes each sentence. The first one is done for you.

1. One green leafy vegetable is
   - ⓐ beans.
   - ⓑ broccoli.
   - ● cabbage.

2. Seeds and fruits are formed by
   - ⓐ bulbs.
   - ⓑ flowers.
   - ⓒ leaves.

3. Places where plants and animals live are called
   - ⓐ environments.
   - ⓑ adaptations.
   - ⓒ deserts.

4. The natural fiber used most in the United States comes from
   - ⓐ rubber trees.
   - ⓑ cotton plants.
   - ⓒ oak trees.

5. Insects are attracted to
   - ⓐ tall plants.
   - ⓑ colorful flowers.
   - ⓒ green leaves.

6. Most paper is made from
   - ⓐ cloth.
   - ⓑ plastic.
   - ⓒ wood.

7. Spines are an adaptation of
   - ⓐ cactus plants.
   - ⓑ poison ivy.
   - ⓒ mushrooms.

8. A plant becomes extinct when every one of its kind has
   - ⓐ moved away.
   - ⓑ died.
   - ⓒ started to grow.

9. An endangered plant is so rare it can only be found growing in
   - ⓐ small numbers.
   - ⓑ large numbers.
   - ⓒ cold areas.

10. Today, much of the rain forest is being
   - ⓐ cut down and burned.
   - ⓑ planted with new trees.
   - ⓒ blown away by the wind.

T17

Mastery Test

Fill in the missing words.

11. The plant that a parasitic plant lives on is called a **host**. (host, acacia)

12. People eat the parts of plants where **food is** stored. (flowers are, food is)

13. Wood is the part of a tree that forms under the **bark**. (leaves, bark)

14. Water, soil, and **minerals** are natural resources. (plastic, minerals)

Use the words below to complete the sentences.

cellophane	elastic	water
chemicals	stem	

15. Because rubber is **elastic**, it can stretch and go back to its original shape.

16. Water is stored in the **stem** and branches of a cactus.

17. Wood pulp is used to make a thin, clear material called **cellophane**.

18. To grow vegetables, you need good soil, plenty of **water**, and the right amount of sunlight.

19. Certain **chemicals** that get into the air and water can harm plants and animals.

Write the answer on the lines.

20. Name the parts of the plant that hold the seeds.
    The parts of a plant that hold the seeds are the fruits.

T18

Just for Fun

Use the clues to complete the puzzle. Choose from the words below.

cells	parasites	pollen	saprophytes
chlorophyll	photosynthesis	reproduce	seeds
fungi	plants	root	spores
oxygen			

Across

2. fungi that live on dead plants
6. the part that holds a plant in the soil
7. a group of living things that can make their own food
8. what many plants use to reproduce
10. the smallest parts of a plant
11. the powder made by male plant parts
12. living things such as molds and mushrooms

Down

1. the green coloring in plant leaves
2. special cells from which fungi reproduce
3. fungi that live on or in living plants or animals
4. a gas given off by plants
5. the way plants make food
9. to make new plants

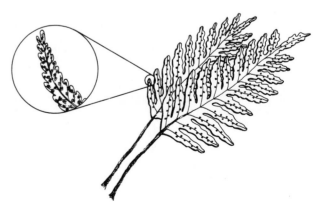

Just for Fun

The following sentences are about flowers. But one word is missing in each sentence. Write in the missing words in the spaces at the right. Choose from the words below.

aster	ovary	sepals
flower	petals	stamens
food	pistil	water
orchid	pollination	wind

1. Maple seeds can travel on the   **W** _ _ _ _ .

2. The female part of a flower is the   _ **I** _ _ _ _ _ .

3. A flower bud is protected by the   _ _ _ _ **L** _ .

4. Vanilla comes from an   _ _ _ _ _ **D** .

5. Insects use nectar for   **F** _ _ _ _ .

6. Moving pollen to the pistil is   _ _ **L** _ _ _ _ _ _ _ _ .

7. The bottom of the pistil is the   **O** _ _ _ _ _ .

8. Seeds are formed inside a   _ _ _ **W** _ _ .

9. The colored parts of a flower are   _ **E** _ _ _ _ .

10. A summer wildflower is an   _ _ _ _ **R** .

11. The male parts of a flower are   **S** _ _ _ _ _ _ .

Just for Fun

The sentences below are about grasses and cereals. But one word is missing from each sentence. Write the words on the spaces at the right. Choose from the words below.

bamboo	grains	rhizomes
blades	lawn grasses	rice
cereal	oats	wheat
chlorophyll		

1. White flour is made from ☐ _ _ _ _ _ .

2. The green material that helps plants make food is _ ☐ _ _ _ _ _ _ _ _ .

3. A food made from plant grains is _ ☐ _ _ _ .

4. The fruits of grass plants are _ _ ☐ _ _ _ .

5. A cereal grain high in protein and vitamins is _ _ ☐ _ .

6. A giant perennial grass is ☐ _ _ _ _ .

7. Grass stems that grow underground are ☐ _ _ _ _ _ _ .

8. A cereal grass that needs a lot of water to grow is _ _ _ ☐ .

9. Grasses that grow thicker when cut are _ ☐ _ _ _ _ _ _ .

10. Spear-shaped grass leaves are _ _ _ ☐ _ _ .

Use the letters in the boxes above to answer the following question.

What can you make with flour? _ _ _ _ _ _ _ _   _ _ _ _ _ _ _

Just for Fun

Use the clues to complete the puzzle. Choose from the words below.

bark	deciduous	palm
coconut	evergreen	taproot
conifer	forest	trunk

Across

2. a kind of tree that loses all its leaves each fall
4. a place where many trees grow
6. the outside of a tree trunk
7. a tree that has leaves shaped like feathers or fans
8. a palm fruit that can float in water
9. the woody stem of a tree

Down

1. a tree that makes seeds in cones
3. a tree that stays green all year
5. a root that grows straight down

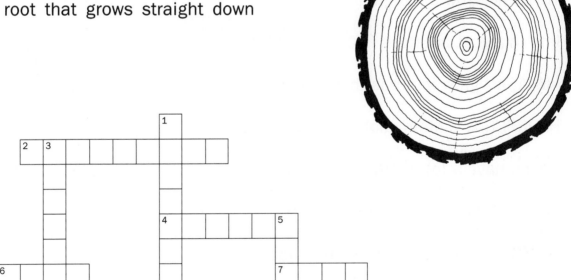

Just for Fun

Each sentence below is about plants used as food. But one word in each sentence is scrambled. Unscramble the letters. Then write the correct word on the lines at the right. Choose from the words below. The first one is done for you.

almonds	carrots	oranges	protein
bananas	lettuce	oregano	rhubarb
cabbage	mineral	peanuts	soybean

1. CUTLETE leaves can be used in salads.

   _ _ _ _ _ _ _
   5

2. YESANOB seeds are rich in protein.

   _ _ _ _ _ _ _
   8

3. GEROSAN grow in areas warm all year long.

   _ _ _ _ _ _ _
   3

4. STROCAR are plant roots.

   _ _ _ _ _ _ _
   4

5. Spaghetti may be flavored with NOOGEAR.

   _ _ _ _ _ _ _
   12

6. TUNSEAP grow underground in pods.

   _ _ _ _ _ _ _
   1

7. Iron in sweet potatoes is a RILNAME.

   _ _ _ _ _ _ _
   11

8. ABNASAN grow in areas that are hot.

   _ _ _ _ _ _ _
   6

9. HARRBUB is a stem cooked for a dessert.

   _ _ _ _ _ _ _
   9

10. Beans have a lot of TREPINO.

    _ _ _ _ _ _ _
    2

11. Food is stored in BAGABEC leaves.

    _ _ _ _ _ _ _
    7

12. DOMSLAN are seeds eaten as nuts.

    _ _ _ _ _ _ _
    10

Solve the Secret Message. When a letter of a word above has a number under it, write that letter above the same number in the Secret Message.

Secret Message: To grow your own vegetables,

_ _ _ _ _ _ _ _ _ _ _ _ .
1 2 3 4 5 6 7 8 9 10 11 12

T24

Just for Fun

Use the clues to complete the puzzle. Choose from the words below.

adaptation	host	pitcher
ants	insects	pollinate
bees	mistletoe	spines
environments		

Across

3. the places where plants and animals live
6. the shape of the leaves of an insect-eating plant
7. a special part of a plant or how a plant lives
8. a plant that a parasitic plant lives on

Down

1. a plant that must get water and minerals from the tree it lives on
2. insects that pollinate colorful flowers
4. what the pitcher plant traps
5. what cactus plants have in place of leaves
7. insects that live on acacia trees

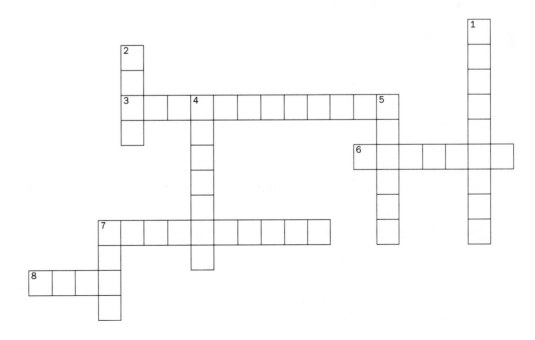

Just for Fun

Each sentence below describes a plant product. But one word in each sentence is scrambled. Unscramble the letters. Then write the correct word on the lines at the right. Choose from the words below.

aspirin	medicines	trunk
cellophane	pine	rubber
cotton		

1. Many plants are used to make DICIMENES. ＿ ＿ ＿ ＿ ＿ ＿ ＿ ＿ ＿

　　　　　　　　　　　　　　　　　　　　　　　　　　　　　　　4

2. A natural fiber made from plants is TTNOOC. ＿ ＿ ＿ ＿ ＿ ＿

3. Car tires are made from a plant product called BUBERR.

   ＿ ＿ ＿ ＿ ＿ ＿

　　　5

4. A type of softwood used to make houses is NEPI. ＿ ＿ ＿ ＿

　　　　　　　　　　　　　　　　　　　　　　　　　　　　　1

5. The bark of the willow tree was once used to make SPINIRA.

   ＿ ＿ ＿ ＿ ＿ ＿ ＿

　2

6. Wood comes from a tree KRUNT. ＿ ＿ ＿ ＿ ＿

7. Wood pulp can be used to make PHANEOCELL.

   ＿ ＿ ＿ ＿ ＿ ＿ ＿ ＿ ＿ ＿

　　　　3

Now solve the Secret Message. When a letter of a word has a number under it, write that letter above the same number in the Secret Message.

Secret Message: You are now writing on a plant product called

＿ ＿ ＿ ＿ ＿ .

1　2　3　4　5

UNIT 8

Just for Fun

Each sentence below describes a way to help protect plants. But one word in each sentence is scrambled. Unscramble the letters. Then write the correct word on the spaces at the right. Choose from the words below.

chemicals	laws	products
environment	plant	resources
forests		

1. People can support the SLAW that we have. __ __ __ __
                                            4

2. People can use HECCAMISL carefully. __ __ __ __ __ __ __ __ __
                                        1

3. People can use plant DUCTSROP wisely. __ __ __ __ __ __ __ __
                                            2

4. People can protect our natural SOCERUSER. __ __ __ __ __ __ __ __ __
                                            6 5

5. Lumber companies can NATPL new trees. __ __ __ __ __
                                            3

6. Areas of land can be set aside as national STOREFS. __ __ __ __ __ __ __
                                                        8

7. People can protect plants and their MERONENVINT.

__ __ __ __ __ __ __ __ __ __ __
   7

Solve the Secret Message. When a letter of a word above has a number under it, write that letter above the same number in the Secret Message.

Secret Message: We should try to __ __ __ __ __ __ __ __ our plants and
                                   1 2 3 4 5 6 7 8
                trees.

UNIT 1 — Just for Fun

Use the clues to complete the puzzle. Choose from the words below.

cells	parasites	pollen	saprophytes
chlorophyll	photosynthesis	reproduce	seeds
fungi	plants	root	spores
oxygen			

Across

2. fungi that live on dead plants
6. the part that holds a plant in the soil
7. a group of living things that can make their own food
8. what many plants use to reproduce
10. the smallest parts of a plant
11. the powder made by male plant parts
12. living things such as molds and mushrooms

Down

1. the green coloring in plant leaves
2. special cells from which fungi reproduce
3. fungi that live on or in living plants or animals
4. a gas given off by plants
5. the way plants make food
9. to make new plants

Crossword answers: SAPROPHYTES, ROOT, PLANTS, SEEDS, CELLS, POLLEN, FUNGI (with down words: CHLOROPHYLL, SPORES, PARASITES, OXYGEN, PHOTOSYNTHESIS, REPRODUCE)

T20

UNIT 2 — Just for Fun

The following sentences are about flowers. But one word is missing in each sentence. Write in the missing words in the spaces at the right. Choose from the words below.

aster	ovary	sepals
flower	petals	stamens
food	pistil	water
orchid	pollination	wind

1. Maple seeds can travel on the **WIND**.
2. The female part of a flower is the **PISTIL**.
3. A flower bud is protected by the **SEPALS**.
4. Vanilla comes from an **ORCHID**.
5. Insects use nectar for **FOOD**.
6. Moving pollen to the pistil is **POLLINATION**.
7. The bottom of the pistil is the **OVARY**.
8. Seeds are formed inside a **FLOWER**.
9. The colored parts of a flower are **PETALS**.
10. A summer wildflower is an **ASTER**.
11. The male parts of a flower are **STAMENS**.

T21

UNIT 3 — Just for Fun

The sentences below are about grasses and cereals. But one word is missing from each sentence. Write the words on the spaces at the right. Choose from the words below.

bamboo	grains	rhizomes
blades	lawn grasses	rice
cereal	oats	wheat
chlorophyll		

1. White flour is made from **WHEAT**.
2. The green material that helps plants make food is **CHLOROPHYLL**.
3. A food made from plant grains is **CEREAL**.
4. The fruits of grass plants are **GRAINS**.
5. A cereal grain high in protein and vitamins is **OATS**.
6. A giant perennial grass is **BAMBOO**.
7. Grass stems that grow underground are **RHIZOMES**.
8. A cereal grass that needs a lot of water to grow is **RICE**.
9. Grasses that grow thicker when cut are **LAWN GRASSES**.
10. Spear-shaped grass leaves are **BLADES**.

Use the letters in the boxes above to answer the following question.

What can you make with flour? **WHEAT** **BREAD**

T22

UNIT 4 — Just for Fun

Use the clues to complete the puzzle. Choose from the words below.

bark	deciduous	palm
coconut	evergreen	taproot
conifer	forest	trunk

Across

2. a kind of tree that loses all its leaves each fall
4. a place where many trees grow
6. the outside of a tree trunk
7. a tree that has leaves shaped like feathers or fans
8. a palm fruit that can float in water
9. the woody stem of a tree

Down

1. a tree that makes seeds in cones
3. a tree that stays green all year
5. a root that grows straight down

Crossword answers: DECIDUOUS, FOREST, BARK, PALM, COCONUT, TRUNK (with down words: CONIFER, EVERGREEN, TAPROOT)

T23

T28

UNIT 5 Just for Fun

Each sentence below is about plants used as food. But one word in each sentence is scrambled. Unscramble the letters. Then write the correct word on the lines at the right. Choose from the words below. The first one is done for you.

almonds	carrots	oranges	protein
bananas	lettuce	oregano	rhubarb
cabbage	mineral	peanuts	soybean

1. CUTLETE leaves can be used in salads. **L E T T U C E**
                                               5

2. YESANOB seeds are rich in protein. **S O Y B E A N**
                                          8

3. GEROSAN grow in areas warm all year long. **O R A N G E S**

4. STROCAR are plant roots. **C A R R O T S**
                               4

5. Spaghetti may be flavored with NOOGEAR. **O R E G A N O**
                                              12

6. TUNSEAP grow underground in pods. **P E A N U T S**
                                         1

7. Iron in sweet potatoes is a RILNAME. **M I N E R A L**
                                           11

8. ABNASAN grow in areas that are hot. **B A N A N A S**
                                           6

9. HARRBUB is a stem cooked for a dessert. **R H U B A R B**
                                              9

10. Beans have a lot of TREPINO. **P R O T E I N**
                                     2

11. Food is stored in BAGABEC leaves. **C A B B A G E**
                                          7

12. DOMSLAN are seeds eaten as nuts. **A L M O N D S**
                                         10

Solve the Secret Message. When a letter of a word above has a number under it, write that letter above the same number in the Secret Message.

Secret Message: To grow your own vegetables,

S T A R T   A   G A R D E N .
 1 2 3 4 5   6   7 8 9 10 11 12

24

UNIT 6 Just for Fun

Use the clues to complete the puzzle. Choose from the words below.

adaptation	host	pitcher
ants	insects	pollinate
bees	mistletoe	spines
environments		

Across
3. the places where plants and animals live
6. the shape of the leaves of an insect-eating plant
7. a special part of a plant or how a plant lives
8. a plant that a parasitic plant lives on

Down
1. a plant that must get water and minerals from the tree it lives on
2. insects that pollinate colorful flowers
4. what the pitcher plant traps
5. what cactus plants have in place of leaves
7. insects that live on acacia trees

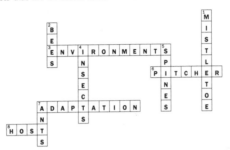

T25

UNIT 7 Just for Fun

Each sentence below describes a plant product. But one word in each sentence is scrambled. Unscramble the letters. Then write the correct word on the lines at the right. Choose from the words below.

aspirin	medicines	trunk
cellophane	pine	rubber
cotton		

Many plants are used to make DICIMENES. **M E D I C I N E S**
                                             4

A natural fiber made from plants is TTNOOC. **C O T T O N**
                                                3

Car tires are made from a plant product called BUBERR.
R U B B E R
 5

A type of softwood used to make houses is NEPI. **P I N E**
                                                   1

The bark of the willow tree was once used to make SPINIRA.
A S P I R I N
 2

Wood comes from a tree KRUNT. **T R U N K**

Wood pulp can be used to make PHANEOCELL.
C E L L O P H A N E
 3

Now solve the Secret Message. When a letter of a word has a number under it, write that letter above the same number in the Secret Message.

Secret Message: You are now writing on a plant product called

P A P E R .
 1 2 3 4 5

26

UNIT 8 Just for Fun

Each sentence below describes a way to help protect plants. But one word in each sentence is scrambled. Unscramble the letters. Then write the correct word on the spaces at the right. Choose from the words below.

chemicals	laws	products
environment	plant	resources
forests		

1. People can support the SLAW that we have. **L A W S**
                                                 4

2. People can use HECCAMISL carefully. **C H E M I C A L S**
                                          1

3. People can use plant DUCTSROP wisely. **P R O D U C T S**
                                             2

4. People can protect our natural SOCERUSER. **R E S O U R C E S**
                                                 6 5

5. Lumber companies can NATPL new trees. **P L A N T**
                                             3

6. Areas of land can be set aside as national STOREFS. **F O R E S T S**
                                                           8

7. People can protect plants and their MERONENVINT.
E N V I R O N M E N T
 7

Solve the Secret Message. When a letter of a word above has a number under it, write that letter above the same number in the Secret Message.

Secret Message: We should try to **C O N S E R V E** our plants and
                                     1 2 3 4 5 6 7 8
trees.

T27

T29

Special Projects

These Special Projects are motivational activities that supplement and provide enrichment to each unit. Read through the projects before beginning a unit to determine when each is most helpful to your class.

UNIT 1 Plants Are Living Things

Mosses Around the World

Materials: encyclopedia

Students may want to research the ways that people in different countries use mosses. (In Ireland decaying deposits of peat moss are used as fuel. In Lapland moss is placed inside cradles to make a soft, warm lining.)

Plant Scrapbook

Materials: notebook, marking pens, camera (optional), glue, field guides

Students may want to start a Plant Scrapbook. They can draw or take pictures of any plant they find interesting and make notes of what they observe about the plant. (They might see flowers, for example, or cones. They might observe that the plant has a woody stem.) Then they can try to identify the plant using a field guide.

UNIT 2 Flowers

State Flowers

Materials: encyclopedia, tracing paper, map

Have students research the flower of your state and several neighboring states. Ask students to draw or trace a map of your state. On the map they should indicate the capital city, the town where they live, and major features such as rivers or mountains. Have students add a drawing of the state flower to the map.

Growing Flowers from Cuttings

Materials: African violet plant (geraniums or begonias can also be used), clay pot, sand, scissors

Students can grow new flowering plants from a cutting. Help them cut one leaf and its stem from an African violet plant (or a geranium or begonia). Place the stem in moist sand in a clay pot. The stem should grow new roots. Then the stem can be transplanted into soil. A new plant will grow from the cutting.

UNIT 3 Grasses and Cereals

Cereals in the United States

Materials: atlas, books on geography or social studies, encyclopedia, colored pencils

Have students trace a map of the United States from an atlas. Then have them use other sources to identify states where wheat, corn, rice, and oats are grown. Students may want to code these states with symbols or color them for the cereal grown there.

Bamboo

Materials: encyclopedia

Ask students to research the uses of bamboo in Asia. Make a master list based on what the students discover. Ask students to think about what materials are used in the United States to make these products.

UNIT 4 Trees

Leaf Identification

Materials: field guide, notebook, blotter paper, wooden board, heavy books, tape

Encourage students to collect leaves from trees in their area. Have them try to identify the trees from their leaves, using a field guide. If they wish, students can preserve the leaves they collect. Place the leaves on a piece of blotter paper and cover them with a second piece. Put a board over the paper and weigh it down with heavy books. When the leaves are completely dry, they can be taped onto the pages of a notebook.

Flowers and Trees

Materials: field guide, poster paper, marking pens

Using a field guide, help students select several kinds of flowering trees. Have them make drawings of the trees and their flowers for a poster. Display the posters in the classroom.

UNIT 5 Plants Used as Food

Class Cookbook

Materials: recipes from students, Class Cookbook started in Unit 3

Ask each student to bring in a recipe that includes one of the foods discussed in the unit. Add these recipes to the Class Cookbook begun in Unit 3.

Nutrition Search

Materials: encyclopedia or books on healthy diet

Encourage students to learn more about vitamins and minerals from an encyclopedia or book on diet and health. Have students make simple tables that list a few of their favorite foods and the vitamins and minerals the foods contain.

UNIT 6 Plant Adaptations

Cactus Terrarium

Materials: small terrarium (or large glass bowl), soil, sand, several desert plants, gravel or small stones

Have students create a miniature desert environment. Place about two inches of potting soil in the terrarium. Add about one inch of sand. Plant several small desert plants. If the plants have spines, handle them with gardening gloves. Cover the soil with gravel or small stones. Place the terrarium in a sunny location. Water the soil about once a week.

Poisonous Plants

Materials: encyclopedia or books on house plants or pets

Have students find out the names of common plants that are poisonous. For example, hyacinth bulbs, mistletoe berries, and the green parts of potatoes are poisonous. Students may also want to consult books on pets to find out what house plants are poisonous to animals.

UNIT 7 Plant Products

Paper Display

Materials: different products made of paper (or pictures of paper products)

Have students make a bulletin board display of the huge variety of products made of paper. Students can make drawings of these products or pin or tape the actual product to the board.

Artificial Fibers

Materials: encyclopedia

Today many of the fibers used to make clothing come from petroleum. Some of these fibers are nylon, polyester, and acrylic. Divide the class into three groups. Ask each group to do research on one of these artificial fibers. Have the students find out what advantages these fibers have. Ask a representative from each group to make a report to the class.

Houses Around the World

Materials: encyclopedia or books on geography or social studies

Let students know that people usually build their homes with the materials that are common and close at hand. This may not always be wood. Native Americans of the Southwest, for example, make homes of adobe, or sun-dried brick, because trees are scarce. Have students do research on the kinds of houses built in different parts of the world. If they wish they can make a bulletin board display showing different styles and materials used.

UNIT 8 Conservation

Keeping Current

Keep any articles you find in newspapers or magazines on the tropical rain forests. Read these articles to the class. Do all the articles agree on how fast the forests are being destroyed? Do they agree on what will happen if the forests are destroyed? Do any of the articles present solutions to the problem? Help students to understand that people in countries such as the United States have an effect on tropical rain forest destruction, even though there are no such forests where they live.

Protect-A-Plant Poster

Materials: poster paper, marking pens

Encourage students to make a poster about the importance of conserving plants. Arrange with a local merchant to display the poster for a time.

Steck Vaughn

WONDERS OF SCIENCE

Plant Life

Joan S. Gottlieb

Rigby • Steck-Vaughn

www.HarcourtAchieve.com
1.800.531.5015

Contents

WONDERS OF SCIENCE

UNIT 1
Plants Are Living Things

Bamboo Plants

Sequoia Tree

What Is a Plant?

Can you imagine grass that can grow as tall as a ten-story building? The grass is called bamboo. Can you picture a tree that has a trunk wide enough to drive a car through? This tree is called a sequoia.

There are five large groups of living things on Earth. The two that you probably know the best are animals and **plants.** Bamboo and sequoias are two kinds of plants. In this book, you will learn about many kinds of plants. The study of plant life is called **botany.**

There are many different kinds of plants. Scientists who study plants put those plants that are alike into groups. It is easier to study groups of plants than to study each plant by itself.

All plants are made up of tiny parts called **cells.** Cells are so small that they cannot be seen without a tool called a **microscope.** Most plants are made of millions of cells.

There are other ways that plants are alike. All plants grow. Plants also have ways to **reproduce.** This means that plants can make new plants just like themselves. Different kinds of plants have different ways to reproduce.

All plants are different from animals in two important ways. First, plants cannot move from place to place as animals do. Also, green plants can make their own food.

A. Write the word or words that best finish each sentence.

1. Bamboo and the sequoia tree are two kinds of _____plants_____ .

2. All plants are made up of parts called _____cells_____ .

3. Cells cannot be seen without a tool called a _____microscope_____ .

4. When plants _____reproduce_____ , they make new plants like themselves.

5. Green plants are living things that can make their own _____food_____ .

6. Plants cannot move from place to place as _____animals_____ do.

B. Answer True or False.

1. There are many different kinds of plants. _____True_____

2. All plants are made up of parts called cells. _____True_____

3. Different kinds of plants have different ways to reproduce. _____True_____

4. Some plants can move from place to place. _____False_____

5. Only a few animals can make their own food. _____False_____

C. Answer the questions.

1. Why do scientists put plants that are alike into groups? _____It is_____ easier to study groups of plants than to study each plant by itself.

2. What are three ways that all plants are alike? _____Answers may_____ vary, but should include: All plants are made up of cells. All plants grow. All plants reproduce. All green plants make their own food.

3. What are two ways that plants are different from animals? _____Plants_____ cannot move from place to place as animals do. Green plants can make their own food.

Parts of a Plant

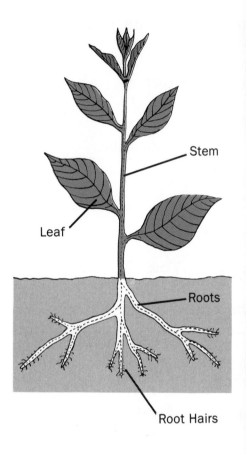

Leaf

Stem

Roots

Root Hairs

Plants are made up of different parts. Most plants have three main parts. The **roots, stems,** and **leaves** help plants to live and grow.

The part of the plant that is in the ground is called the root. Some plants have only one main root. Other plants have roots that are branched. Roots hold plants in the soil. The roots of some plants store food. The root of the carrot plant stores food.

The tips of roots are covered with tiny **root hairs.** These root hairs take in water from the soil. The water and soil contain **minerals.** Minerals are substances that plants need to grow. The water that is taken in by the root hairs carries the needed minerals.

The stem is the part of a plant that helps hold up the plant. The stem carries water and minerals from the roots of the plant up to the leaves. The stem also carries food from the leaves down to the roots.

The part of the plant that is easiest to see is its leaves. Most plants have green leaves. The material that makes leaves green is chlorophyll. **Chlorophyll** helps plants make food.

On the underside of a leaf are many tiny openings. Air enters through these openings. The leaves use a gas from the air to help make food. The gas is called **carbon dioxide.** The leaves give off another gas called **oxygen** into the air. People and other animals take in oxygen when they breathe.

A. **Answer True or False.**

1. Most plants have three main parts. _____True_____

2. A plant's leaves carry water to the roots. _____False_____

3. Chlorophyll helps plants make food. _____True_____

4. Roots hold plants in the soil. _____True_____

5. Stems give off carbon dioxide into the air. _____False_____

6. Some plants have roots that are branched. _____True_____

7. Root hairs take in oxygen from the air. _____False_____

B. **Use each word to write a sentence about plants.**

1. roots _____ Sentences will vary. _____

   _____

2. leaves _____

   _____

3. stem _____

   _____

C. **Answer the questions.**

1. What are the three main parts of a plant? _____The three main_____
   _____parts are the roots, the stem, and the leaves._____

   _____

2. What gas from the air do leaves use? _____The leaves use_____
   _____a gas called carbon dioxide._____

3. What gas do leaves give off? _____Leaves give off a gas_____
   _____called oxygen._____

4. What is the material that makes leaves green? _____The material_____
   _____that makes leaves green is chlorophyll._____

Plants Make Food

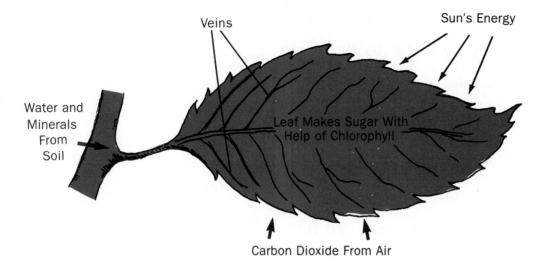

Veins

Sun's Energy

Water and Minerals From Soil

Leaf Makes Sugar With Help of Chlorophyll

Carbon Dioxide From Air

A leaf makes its own food.

Green plants can do something that you cannot do. Green plants can make their own food. People get food from plants or from animals that eat plants.

The way that plants make food is called **photosynthesis.** Chlorophyll in the plant's leaves takes in energy from the sun. The leaves use the energy to make sugar from carbon dioxide and water. Plants also make fats, proteins, and vitamins. These materials are important for your health. That is why plants are good for you to eat.

The plant lives on the sugar it makes. Sugar that the plant does not use right away is changed into a food called starch. Starch is stored in different parts of the plant. In carrot plants, starch is stored in the root. In cabbages, the starch is stored in the leaves. Food is stored in the stems of celery plants. Animals and people eat the different parts of many plants that store food.

Some plants that live in cold areas lose their leaves in the fall. These plants cannot make food in the winter. They live on their stored food. Other plants do not lose their leaves in the fall. These plants are called **evergreens.** Their leaves are often shaped like needles.

A. **Use the words below to complete the sentences.**

chlorophyll	oxygen	starch
food	photosynthesis	water

1. Green plants can make their own _____food_____ .

2. The way that plants make food is called _____photosynthesis_____ .

3. The ____chlorophyll____ in a plant's leaves takes in energy from the sun.

4. Leaves make sugar from carbon dioxide and _____water_____ .

5. Sugar that the plant does not use right away is changed into
_____starch_____ .

B. **Answer <u>True</u> or <u>False</u>.**

1. People do not get food from plants. ____False____

2. Green plants cannot make their own food. ____False____

3. Starch is stored in different parts of a plant. ____True____

4. Plants make fats, proteins, and vitamins. ____True____

5. A plant lives on the sugar it makes. ____True____

6. Animals and people only eat plant roots. ____False____

C. **Answer the questions.**

1. What is photosynthesis? ____Photosynthesis is the way that____
____plants make food.____

2. What happens to the sugar that a plant does not use right away?
____The sugar that the plant does not use right away____
____is changed into a food called starch.____

3. Where do people get food? ____People get food from plants or____
____from animals that eat plants.____

How Plants Reproduce

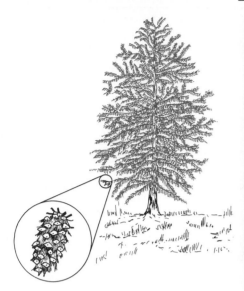

Pine Tree and Cone

Strawberry Plant With Runner

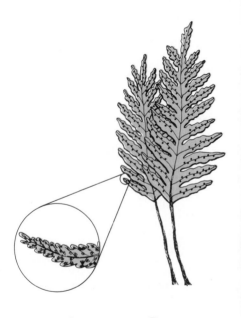

Spores on a Fern

All living things must have a way to reproduce, or make new living things just like themselves. Different plants have different ways to reproduce.

Many plants reproduce from **seeds.** There are two kinds of seed plants. Evergreen plants, like pine trees, make seeds in <u>cones.</u> Flowering plants, such as apple trees, make seeds in flowers.

Seed plants have female parts where seeds grow. The male parts make a powder called **pollen**. Often bees or other insects carry pollen to the female parts. The pollen **fertilizes** the female parts. This means that the pollen enters the female cells. The fertilized female cells make seeds.

Each seed has a tiny new plant inside. Some seeds just fall from the plant to the soil. Maple tree seeds and dandelion seeds are carried far by the wind. Other seeds have coverings that can stick to an animal's fur. When the seeds drop onto moist soil, they grow into new plants.

Some plants can reproduce from parts of themselves. Strawberry plants have stems that run along the ground. These stems can grow roots and make new plants. Many grasses reproduce in the same way. Their stems run underground and can also make new plants.

Mosses and ferns reproduce from **spores.** Spores are special cells that can live a long time without water. When spores do get enough water, they grow into new plants.

A. Use each word to write a sentence about plants.

1. seeds _____ Sentences will vary. _____

_____

2. cones _____

_____

3. pollen _____

_____

B. Fill in the missing words.

1. Different plants have different ways to _____reproduce_____ .
   (make food, reproduce)

2. Each seed has a tiny new ___plant___ inside. (plant, spore)

3. Pine trees make seeds in ___cones___ . (flowers, cones)

4. Apple trees make seeds in ___flowers___ . (flowers, cones)

5. Strawberry plants have ___stems___ that run along the ground and
   make new plants. (stems, leaves)

6. Mosses and ferns reproduce from ___spores___ . (pollen, spores)

C. Answer the questions.

1. What are three ways that plants reproduce? _____Plants_____
   _____reproduce from seeds, from stems running_____
   _____along the ground or underground, or from spores._____

   _____

2. What are spores? _____Spores are special cells that can_____
   _____live a long time without water._____

3. The male parts of seed plants make pollen. What does pollen do?
   _____The pollen fertilizes the female parts._____

   _____

How Plants Are Grouped

Bean Plant

Daisy

Lilac

Maple Tree

Plants can be grouped in many ways. There are plants with flowers and plants with cones. There are plants with wide, flat leaves and other plants with needlelike leaves. Scientists put plants into groups with other plants most like them in certain ways.

One important group is made up of plants that have **tubes.** The tubes are made of cells and act like drinking straws. The tubes begin in the roots, run through the stem, and end in the leaves. They carry water and minerals from the soil to the leaves for food production. The tubes also carry food from the leaves to other parts of the plant.

Plants with tubes are often taller than plants without tubes. The tubes can carry materials throughout even the tallest plants. Plants without tubes are usually smaller. They often grow in or near water. Algae and mosses are plants that do not have tubes.

Plants with tubes have different kinds of stems. Some have soft stems that bend easily. Bean plants and daisies have soft stems. Plants with soft stems usually do not grow very large. Their soft stems do not live more than one or two growing seasons. Some grasses are also in this group.

Other plants with tubes have thick, woody stems. Woody stems are strong and do not bend easily. Bushes and trees have woody stems. Woody stems can grow taller and thicker each year. They may live for hundreds of years.

A. Underline the correct words.

1. There are (two ways, eight ways, <u>many ways</u>) to group plants.

2. Some plants with tubes are (algae, <u>daisies</u>, mosses).

3. Plants without tubes often grow in or near (sand, <u>water</u>).

4. (<u>Bean plants</u>, Bushes, Trees) have soft stems.

5. (<u>Bushes and trees</u>, Daisies) have woody stems.

B. Use the words below to complete the sentences.

algae	roots	tubes
mosses	soft	woody

1. Water and minerals are carried from the soil to the leaves by
   <u>tubes</u> .

2. The tubes of a plant begin in the <u>roots</u> .

3. Two kinds of plants that do not have tubes are <u>algae</u> and
   <u>mosses</u> .

4. Trees have <u>woody</u> stems that grow taller and thicker each
   year.

5. Plants with <u>soft</u> stems usually do not grow very large.

C. Answer the questions.

1. How do scientists put plants into groups? <u>Scientists put</u>
   <u>plants into groups with other plants most like</u>
   <u>them in certain ways.</u>

2. What do the tubes in a plant do for the plant? <u>They carry water</u>
   <u>and minerals from the soil to the leaves. They carry</u>
   <u>food from the leaves to other parts of the plant.</u>
   _____

Plantlike Organisms

Fungi

Fungi on a Log

There are living things that are like plants in many ways. They grow and reproduce. But they are different in one important way. They cannot make their own food like plants can.

One group of these living things is called **fungi.** Some fungi live on or in other living plants or animals. These fungi are called **parasites.** Other fungi live on dead plant matter and dead animals. These fungi are called **saprophytes.** All fungi get food from the things they live on.

Many fungi grow in dark, damp places. Fungi cause dead things to rot. Rotting things turn into soil, making soil richer for growing plants.

Like some plants, fungi reproduce from spores. When conditions are right, the spores grow into new fungi.

A. Fill in the missing words.

1. Fungi that live on or in other living plants or animals are called

   _____parasites_____. (saprophytes, parasites)

2. Fungi that live on dead plant matter or dead animals are

   called _____saprophytes_____. (saprophytes, parasites)

3. Fungi reproduce from ___spores___. (seeds, spores)

B. Answer the question.

Fungi cannot make their own food. How do fungi get their food? _____

Fungi get food from the things they live on.

14

Plantlike Organisms

Molds

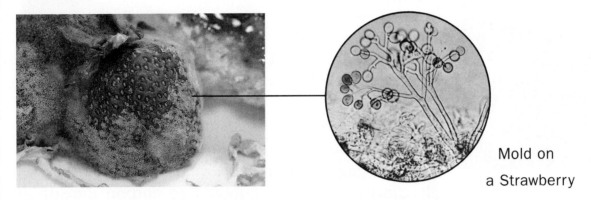

Mold on
a Strawberry

Have you ever seen an orange or a slice of bread with a fuzzy blue-green spot? The fuzzy spot is a kind of fungi called a **mold.** Like the rest of the fungi group, molds cannot make their own food. Molds get their food from the things they live on. Molds grow on fruit, bread, cheese, and even leather.

Molds reproduce from spores. As new molds grow, they cause the food they are growing on to spoil, or rot. Sometimes, it is not harmful to eat foods with mold. But usually, it is better to throw moldy food away.

There are molds that are useful to people. Have you ever heard of penicillin? This life-saving medicine is made from a mold. A mold gives blue cheese a flavor that many people like. The blue part of the cheese is the mold.

Answer the questions.

1. How do molds get their food? _____ Molds get their food from the things they live on.

2. How are molds useful to people? _____ A mold gives blue cheese its flavor. A life-saving medicine is also made from a mold.

15

Plantlike Organisms

Yeasts

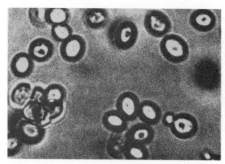

Yeast Cells

Yeast is used to make some breads rise.

Did you know that your favorite bread is made with living cells? They are **yeast** cells. Yeast is part of the fungi group. Like other fungi, it cannot make its own food. Yeast cells live on the sugar in foods, such as fruits and grains. As yeast uses sugar to grow, it gives off carbon dioxide gas. The bubbles of carbon dioxide from yeast make bread light and fluffy.

The small, round yeast cell reproduces very quickly. As a yeast cell grows, it forms a bulge, called a **bud.** The bud grows into a new yeast cell. Then the new cell forms a bud, and so on. The cells quickly multiply and form a group of yeast cells. The group splits into more groups.

A. Answer True or False.

1. Yeast is part of the fungi group. _____True_____

2. Yeast cells live on the sugar in foods. _____True_____

3. As a yeast cell grows, it forms a spore. _____False_____

4. Yeast cells reproduce very slowly. _____False_____

B. Answer the questions.

1. What gas is given off as yeast uses sugar to grow? _____Yeast_____
    gives off carbon dioxide gas.

2. How does a yeast cell grow? _____It forms a bulge called a bud._____
    The bud grows into a new yeast cell.

Plantlike Organisms

Mushrooms

Have you ever eaten a pizza with **mushrooms?** Mushrooms are also in the fungi group. The kind of mushrooms you find in a supermarket are safe to eat. But many mushrooms that grow in the wild are poisonous. These poisonous mushrooms are sometimes called toadstools.

Two parts of a mushroom grow above the ground. The stemlike part is called the **stalk.** On top of the stalk is the **cap.** The cap looks like an umbrella. Spores are made underneath the cap. The spores may fall onto the ground or be carried by the wind. New mushrooms grow from the spores.

A mushroom has threadlike roots that grow underground. These roots take in food for the mushroom.

Most mushrooms are saprophytes. They live on dead matter in the soil.

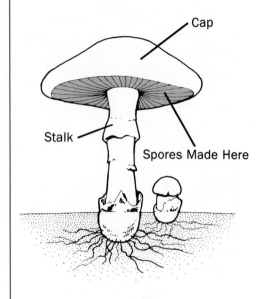

Mushroom

A. **Underline the correct words.**

1. Mushrooms are in the (flower, animal, fungi) group.

2. Most mushrooms are (saprophytes, toadstools, flowers).

3. The stemlike part of a mushroom is the (cap, stalk, spore).

4. Poisonous mushrooms are sometimes called (saprophytes, toadstools).

5. New mushrooms grow from (fungi, spores).

B. **Answer the question.**

What do mushrooms live on? _____ They live on dead matter in the soil.

Plants Without Tubes

Algae

A Kind of Seaweed Called Kelp

Remember that plants can be grouped in many ways. Some plants have tubes and others grow without tubes. **Algae** are plants that do not have tubes.

Most algae live in oceans, lakes, and ponds. They float on the water or grow on the ocean floor. But some can grow in soil, and others grow on tree bark.

Some algae are made up of only one cell. Others are large plants called seaweed.

All algae have chlorophyll and can make their own food. But some algae do not look green. Some may look red or brown.

Algae are important to water animals. They give off oxygen into the water. Water animals take in the oxygen and also feed on the algae.

A. **Answer True or False.**

1. Algae are plants that do not have tubes. _____True_____

2. Algae cannot make their own food. _____False_____

3. Most algae grow in soil. _____False_____

B. **Answer the question.**

What are two reasons why algae are important to water animals? _____

Algae give off oxygen into the water. Water animals

take in the oxygen and feed on the algae.

Plants Without Tubes

Mosses

Mosses

Millions of years ago, giant **mosses** grew in great forests on Earth. Mosses living today are very small plants that do not have tubes.

Mosses have chlorophyll and make their own food. But they do not need much sunlight. Mosses grow best in warm, shady, wet places. Some mosses live in water. Others live high in trees. Mosses that grow on soil make a thick carpetlike covering. This covering helps hold soil in place. As mosses die and break down, they help make soil richer.

Mosses reproduce in two stages. First, male and female cells join to form a tiny plant. The tiny plant then makes spores. When the weather is warm and wet, the spores grow into new plants.

A. Answer <u>True</u> or <u>False</u>.

1. Mosses make their own food. _____True_____

2. Mosses have tubes. _____False_____

3. As mosses die and break down, they help make soil richer. _____True_____

B. Answer the question.

Where do mosses grow best? _____Mosses grow best in warm, shady, wet places._____

Plants with Tubes

Ferns and Seed Plants

Fern

Daffodil

Most plants with tubes are either **ferns** or seed plants. All ferns and seed plants have leaves, stems, and roots. So they are sometimes called true plants.

Ferns grow in wet, shady places in most parts of the world. Some ferns are as small as a moss plant. Others can grow to be as tall as a tree.

Only the leaves of most ferns can be seen. The stems of most ferns grow under the ground.

Ferns do not have flowers or seeds. They reproduce with spores. The spores form on the underside of the leaves.

Most common plants have flowers. The flowers make seeds, and the plants reproduce from these seeds. You will read more about seed plants and other kinds of plants in the following units.

A. **Fill in the missing words.**

1. Most plants with tubes are either _____ferns_____ or seed plants. (ferns, flowers)

2. Ferns reproduce with ____spores____. (spores, tubes)

3. Only the ____leaves____ of most ferns can be seen. (leaves, stems)

B. **Answer the questions.**

1. What kinds of plants have tubes? _____Most plants with tubes are_____ _____either ferns or seed plants._____

2. Why are ferns and seed plants sometimes called true plants? _____All_____ _____ferns and seed plants have leaves, stems, and roots._____

Part A

Use the words below to complete the sentences.

buds	flowers	photosynthesis
cells	leaves	spores
chlorophyll	oxygen	true

1. Plants are made up of tiny parts called _____cells_____ .

2. The three main parts of a plant are roots, stems, and _____leaves_____ .

3. Flowering plants make seeds in _____flowers_____ .

4. Leaves give off _____oxygen_____ into the air.

5. The way that plants make food is called _____photosynthesis_____ .

6. Mosses and ferns reproduce from _____spores_____ .

7. Yeasts reproduce by growing _____buds_____ .

8. All algae have _____chlorophyll_____ and make their own food.

9. Ferns and seed plants are called _____true_____ plants.

Part B

Read each sentence. Write <u>True</u> if the sentence is true. Write <u>False</u> if the sentence is false.

1. All plants grow, reproduce, and make their own food. ____True____

2. Plants can be grouped in only one way. ____False____

3. The material that makes leaves green is chlorophyll. ____True____

4. Fungi reproduce from spores. ____True____

5. Molds can make their own food. ____False____

6. Mushrooms live on dead matter in the soil. ____True____

7. Ferns have flowers and seeds. ____False____

8. True plants have roots, stems, and leaves. ____True____

EXPLORE & DISCOVER

Plant Parts We Eat

You Need

- poster paper
- scissors
- old magazines
- markers
- glue
- encyclopedia or gardening guides

1. We eat the roots, stems, leaves, flowers, fruits, and seeds of plants. On a large sheet of poster paper make a chart like the one in the diagram.

2. To fill each box on the chart, find pictures of fruits and vegetables in old magazines.

3. You can also draw foods on a piece of paper. Cut out the pictures or drawings.

4. Put each food in its correct box on the poster paper. Use gardening guides or encyclopedias to find out the plant part.

5. Glue your pictures to the chart, and label each food.

Plant Parts We Eat

Plant Parts	Foods 
Roots	
Stems	
Leaves	
Fruits	
Seeds	

Write the Answer

Which part of a plant do you eat most often?

Answers will vary but should include the name of the

parts—root, stem, leaf, or flower—and the food itself.

The plant part I eat most often is the leaf. I eat lots of spinach and lettuce.

22

Fill in the circle in front of the word or phrase that best completes each sentence. The first one is done for you.

1. All plants are made of
   - ⓐ fungi.
   - ⓑ spores.
   - ● cells.

2. Roots, stems, and leaves are the main parts of
   - ⓐ an animal.
   - ⓫ a plant.
   - ⓒ fungi.

3. The way plants make food is called
   - ⓐ photosynthesis.
   - ⓑ reproducing.
   - ⓒ budding.

4. Chlorophyll in a plant's leaves takes in energy from
   - ⓐ the wind.
   - ⓫ the sun.
   - ⓒ pollen.

5. Fungi that live on dead plants are
   - ⓐ saprophytes.
   - ⓑ pollen.
   - ⓒ spores.

6. Some plants that do not have tubes are
   - ⓐ trees and bushes.
   - ⓫ mosses and algae.
   - ⓒ daisies and beans.

Fill in the missing words.

7. Some evergreen plants grow seeds in _____cones_____. (spores, cones)

8. A mold is a kind of _____fungi_____. (animal, fungi)

9. Yeast cells live on _____sugar_____. (sugar, pollen)

Write the answer on the lines.

10. How do water and minerals move from the soil to the leaves of a plant?
    Tubes carry water and minerals
    from the soil to the leaves of the plant.

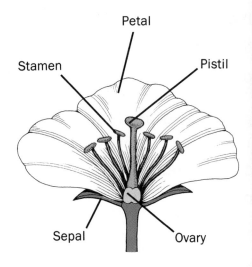

Petal

Stamen

Pistil

Sepal

Ovary

Pistil   Stamens   Petal

The Parts of a Flower

When you think of a flower, you might imagine colored petals and a nice smell. But flowers are more than just pretty to look at and pleasant to smell. They are important parts of seed plants. Flowers make the seeds that plants reproduce from.

Look at the drawing of the flower. Find the **sepals.** Sepals are green and look like leaves. They protect the flower when it is a bud.

Flower **petals** have many shapes, sizes, and colors. Their bright colors and smells help bring different kinds of animals to the flowers. Many flowers attract insects. Others attract birds. Some even attract bats!

Many flowers have both male and female parts. The male parts are the **stamens.** A powder called **pollen** is made in the top part of the stamens.

The female part of the flower is the **pistil.** The top of the pistil is sticky. If pollen grains land on the pistil, they stay there. Then the pollen grows a tube down into the **ovary.** The ovary is at the bottom of the pistil.

In the ovary, male cells from the pollen tube join egg cells, or **ovules.** The pollen cells fertilize the ovules. The fertilized cells start to form seeds. The ovary develops into a **fruit.** A fruit holds the seeds that form in the flower. A fruit can be soft and fleshy, like a peach. Or it can be hard, like a walnut.

A. **Draw lines to complete the sentences.**

1. Petals have many   in the top part of the stamens.

2. Pollen is made   down into the ovary.

3. The pistil is   shapes, sizes, and colors.

4. Pollen grows a tube   the female part of the flower.

B. **Label the parts of a flower. Use the words below.**

| ovary | pistil | stamen |
| petal | sepal | |

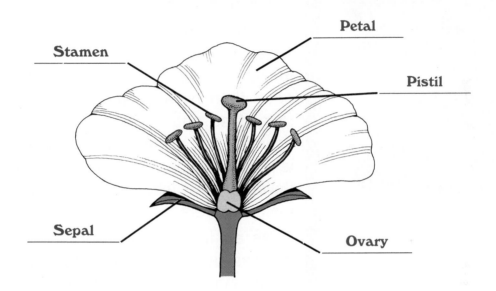

Petal

Stamen

Pistil

Sepal

Ovary

C. **Answer the questions.**

1. What is made in the top part of the stamens? _____ A _____

   powder called pollen is made in the top part of the stamens.

2. What happens to pollen grains that stick on the pistil? _____

   The pollen grows a tube down into the ovary.

3. What do fertilized cells start to form in the ovary? _____ The _____

   fertilized cells start to form seeds.

4. What does a fruit hold? _____ A fruit holds the _____

   seeds that form in the flower.

Pollination

Many flowers are pollinated by bees.

For seeds to form, pollen from the male part of a flower has to reach the female part. Moving pollen from the stamens of a flower to the pistil is called **pollination.** A flower may get pollen from its own stamens. It can also get pollen from another flower.

Pollination can take place in many ways. The wind can carry pollen. Trees and grasses are often pollinated by the wind. Wind can carry pollen as far as 100 miles from a plant!

Flowers that are brightly colored or that have strong smells are often pollinated by insects. More flowers are pollinated by bees than by any other kind of insect. Butterflies and moths are attracted to flowers that make a lot of **nectar.** Nectar is a sweet liquid that is made inside a flower. Some insects feed on the nectar inside flowers.

As an insect moves around in a flower, it picks up pollen from the stamens. Some of the pollen rubs off on the pistil. The flower is pollinated. Suppose the insect flies to another flower. It may still have pollen on its body. Then the pollen can rub off onto the pistil of the second flower. In that way, the second flower is pollinated.

Banana flowers open only at night. How are they pollinated? Some bats are active at night and feed on nectar. So when the banana flowers open, bats are there to feed on them. Then the flowers are pollinated.

A. Answer True or False.

1. All flowers are pollinated by bees. _____False_____

2. Colors and smells may attract insects to flowers. _____True_____

3. When pollen reaches the pistil of a flower, pollination takes place.
_____True_____

4. The wind cannot carry pollen. _____False_____

5. Some insects feed on nectar inside flowers. _____True_____

B. Fill in the missing words.

1. Moving pollen to the pistil of a flower is called
_____pollination_____. (photosynthesis, pollination)

2. Grasses are often pollinated by the _____wind_____. (wind, bees)

3. Flowers that are brightly colored are often pollinated by
_____insects_____. (wind, insects)

4. _____Bats_____ pollinate flowers that open at night. (Bats, People)

5. In pollination, pollen moves from the stamens to a _____pistil_____.
(pistil, petal)

C. Answer the questions.

1. What is pollination? _____Pollination is moving pollen from_____
_____the stamens of a flower to the pistil._____

2. What are two ways that flowers can be pollinated? _____Flowers_____
_____can be pollinated by the wind. They can also be_____
_____pollinated by insects and bats._____

3. How does an insect help pollination take place? _____As an insect_____
_____moves around inside a flower, it picks up pollen from the stamens._____
_____Then the pollen rubs off on the pistil._____

How Seeds Travel

Maple Seed

Dandelion

Burrs

What would happen if all the seeds a flower made fell on the soil right next to the plant? All the seeds might start to grow. But soon there would not be enough water, minerals, or sunlight for all the young plants.

Instead of landing next to the plant, some seeds travel before they fall onto the soil. How do seeds travel? The wind can carry seeds. The fluffy seeds of a dandelion float on the wind. They travel far from the flower that made them. Maple trees also have seeds that travel on the wind.

Animals can help seeds travel. Have you ever seen a dog with burrs in its coat? Burrs are seeds with sharp spines. The spines catch onto an animal's fur. Then the seeds may drop off far from the plant.

Birds and other animals help seeds travel, too. Birds eat fruits like cherries. The seeds, or pits, of the fruit are not digested in the bird's body. Instead, they pass through and drop on the ground with the bird's wastes. Then the seeds can begin to grow.

In the fall, squirrels begin to collect acorns. Acorns are the seeds of oak trees. Squirrels bury the acorns and use them as food in the winter. But squirrels may not find all the acorns they have hidden. They may not eat all the acorns they have stored. So some of the acorns that are hidden in soil will begin to grow into new oak trees.

A. Answer True or False.

1. All seeds grow next to the plant that made them. _____False_____

2. Some seeds are carried by the wind. _____True_____

3. Birds digest the seeds they eat. _____False_____

4. Animals like squirrels help seeds travel. _____True_____

5. Some seeds can travel on an animal's fur. _____True_____

B. Choose the word or words that best match the way each seed travels.

animal fur	birds	squirrels	wind

1. acorns _____squirrels_____

2. cherries _____birds_____

3. burrs _____animal fur_____

4. maple seeds _____wind_____

C. Which seed might travel on the wind? Write the word <u>wind</u> on the line below the seed.

Dandelion   Acorn   Burr

_____wind_____   _____   _____

D. Answer the question.

What would happen if all seeds grew next to the plant that made

them? _____There would not be enough water, minerals, or_____

_____sunlight for all the young plants._____

29

Daisies

Daisies

You may see daisies growing wild in fields or planted in gardens. Daisies are easy to grow, and there are many different kinds. From spring until late fall, one type of daisy or another is blooming. Daisies are plants that can grow year after year. They are **perennials.**

Daisies can grow from seeds. But the seeds grow slowly. So, many people grow daisies from young plants instead.

Depending on the kind of daisy, a daisy plant may grow to be 12 to 36 inches high. The flowers grow on long stems. Many daisy flowers are white with yellow or orange centers. Some are pink. Some kinds of daisies have one layer of petals. Others have two.

Daisies can grow in almost any kind of soil, as long as it is well drained. Wet winter soil can kill a daisy.

A. **Answer True or False.**

1. Daisy seeds grow quickly. ___False___

2. Daisies are perennials. ___True___

3. Daisies can live in almost any soil that is well drained. ___True___

4. Daisy flowers bloom only in the spring. ___False___

B. **Answer the question.**

How would you describe daisy flowers? ___Answers may vary, but should include: The flowers grow on long stems. Many are white with yellow or orange centers, but some are pink. Some have one layer of petals. Others have two.___

Tulips

Tulips

When people see tulips, they often think of Holland. That country grows more than 2,000 kinds of tulips.

Tulips are perennials. They can grow from seeds. But it may take four to seven years for tulips to make flowers. So most tulips are grown from **bulbs.** A bulb is a kind of underground stem with leaves that store food. Onions are bulbs that can be eaten.

Tulip bulbs are planted in the fall. In the early spring, the leaves and stems begin to grow. The leaves are long and pointed. There is usually only one flower on a stem.

Tulip flowers are shaped like a bell or cup. Most have six petals. But some can have double rows of petals. Tulips are found in many different bright colors. Some tulips have petals with streaks of color.

A. Draw lines to complete the sentences.

1. Tulip leaves — have six petals.

2. Most tulip flowers — from bulbs.

3. Tulips are grown mostly — are long and pointed.

B. Answer the questions.

1. What is a bulb? _____ A bulb is a kind of underground stem with leaves that store food.

2. When do tulips begin to grow? _____ Leaves and stems begin to grow in early spring.

Violets

You can see violets growing in woods, in fields, and along the side of the road. Violets grow wild. They can also be grown in gardens. Violets grow best in damp soil.

There are more than 500 kinds of violets. Most are perennials. They can grow for many years. Most violet plants have leaves that are shaped like hearts. The bird's-foot violet has leaves that are shaped like a bird's foot.

Violets grow from an underground stem that lives through the winter. In the spring, the new plants grow and make flowers. Some violets have blue or purple flowers. All violet flowers have five petals.

Violets are found all over the world. They are sometimes used to make dyes, perfumes, and medicines.

Violets

A. Answer True or False.

1. All violet flowers have five petals. _____True_____

2. Violets grow best in dry soil. _____False_____

3. Many violets have leaves that are shaped like hearts. _____True_____

B. Answer the questions.

1. Where can you see violets growing? _____You can see violets in woods, in fields, along the side of the road, and in gardens._____

2. What do violets grow from? _____Violets grow from an underground stem that lives through the winter._____

Wildflowers

You may see flowers along a path in a forest. You may also see them along the side of the road or in an empty lot. People did not plant these flowers. They are **wildflowers** and have probably been growing on their own for years.

Many wildflowers are **annual** plants. Annuals live for just one year. New plants grow from the seeds made by the plants. If you pick the flowers of annual wildflowers, there will be fewer seeds to make new plants next year. So it is best not to pick any wildflowers. Let them grow and make new plants that everyone can enjoy.

People have destroyed many of the places where wildflowers grew. Now many kinds are hard to find. But there are laws to protect them.

A. Answer <u>True</u> or <u>False</u>.

1. Wildflowers are not planted by people. ____True____

2. Some kinds of wildflowers are protected by law. ____True____

B. Answer the question.

Why is it best not to pick annual wildflowers? ____If you pick____ the flowers, there will be fewer seeds to make new plants.

Orchids

Orchids

Vanilla Orchid

You may think of orchids as beautiful flowers that grow in the jungle. Many kinds of orchids do grow in hot, damp climates. But some grow in cool woods and others grow in swamps. In cool places, orchids grow on the ground. They grow from thick, fleshy roots and come up year after year. In hot places, orchids grow high in the branches of trees. Their seeds are carried into the trees by the wind. As the plants grow, they send out roots along the branches of the tree. The roots hold the orchid plants tightly to the branches.

Orchid flowers are found in many shapes, sizes, and colors. Some flowers are tiny. Others may be 10 inches across. Some orchids have wonderful smells, while others have bad smells.

The shape of an orchid flower helps attract the special bird or insect that pollinates the flower. One flower petal is shaped like a scoop and is called a lip. Marks on the lip act as guides for an insect. They show the way into the flower. The insect feeds on the nectar inside the flower. The orchid gets pollinated as the insect moves around inside the flower.

Most orchids are grown for their beautiful flowers. People often wear them for special occasions. But one kind of orchid is a food plant. It is called the vanilla orchid. Vanilla flavoring comes from its seedpods. Vanilla is used to flavor foods such as cakes and ice cream.

A. Answer True or False.

1. Orchids grow only in hot, damp places. ___False___

2. All orchid flowers are tiny. ___False___

3. Some orchids grow from thick, fleshy roots. ___True___

4. Some orchid flowers are pollinated by insects. ___True___

5. Most orchids are grown for food. ___False___

6. In hot places, orchids grow in tree branches. ___True___

7. All orchid flowers have wonderful smells. ___False___

B. Fill in the missing words.

1. Marks on the lip of an orchid help guide ___insects___. (people, insects)

2. In cool places, orchids grow ___on the ground___. (on the ground, in trees)

3. A food that comes from orchids is ___vanilla___. (vanilla, cocoa)

4. Most orchids are grown for their ___flowers___. (flowers, pods)

5. Insects get ___nectar___ from orchid flowers. (vanilla, nectar)

6. The ___shape___ of an orchid flower helps attract the special bird or insect that pollinates the flower. (shape, pods)

C. Answer the questions.

1. Where do orchids grow? ___They grow in hot, damp climates.___
   ___They grow in cool woods. They grow in swamps.___

2. How does an orchid flower get pollinated? ___It gets pollinated___
   ___as an insect moves around inside the flower.___

3. Why are most orchids grown? ___Most orchids are grown___
   ___for their beautiful flowers.___

35

Asters

Aster

Asters are wildflowers that grow almost anywhere. Some cover roadsides and meadows. Some grow in salt marshes and in woods. Others grow in dry, sandy soil. Asters can also be grown as garden flowers.

There are more than 200 kinds of asters. Some are only a few inches high, while others grow many feet high. The flowers can be tiny or very large. Some asters have many flowers on each stem. The flowers can be pink, purple, blue, or white. Most asters bloom in late summer.

An aster may look like a single flower, but it is really many flowers. At the center of an aster are yellow <u>disk</u> flowers. The disk flowers make seeds. Around the disk flowers are <u>ray</u> flowers. Ray flowers look like petals. They do not make seeds.

A. Answer <u>True</u> or <u>False</u>.

1. Asters are wildflowers. ____True____

2. Asters bloom in the spring. ____False____

B. Answer the questions.

1. Where do asters grow? _____ They grow along roadsides and in meadows. They grow in salt marshes, in woods, and in dry, sandy soil. They are also grown in gardens.

2. An aster is made of two kinds of flowers. What is the difference between them? ____ One makes seeds. The other doesn't.

Part A

Use the words below to complete the sentences.

bulbs	petals	pollination
egg cells	pistil	sepals
ovary	pollen	stamens

1. The _____petals_____ help bring different kinds of animals to flowers.

2. The male parts of flowers are the _____stamens_____ .

3. The female part of a flower is the _____pistil_____ .

4. The male parts of a flower make _____pollen_____ .

5. In the ovary of a flower, male cells from the pollen tube join with _____egg cells_____ .

6. The _____ovary_____ develops into a fruit.

7. Flower buds are protected by small green _____sepals_____ .

8. Moving pollen from the stamen of a flower to the pistil is called _____pollination_____ .

Part B

Underline the correct words.

1. Flowers with bright colors and nice smells are usually pollinated by (<u>insects</u>, bats).

2. Insects get (vanilla, <u>nectar</u>) from flowers.

3. Maple trees have seeds that can be carried by (<u>the wind</u>, squirrels).

4. Flowers that people do not plant are called (petunias, <u>wildflowers</u>).

5. Tulips grow from (<u>bulbs</u>, roots).

6. An example of a wildflower is (a tulip, <u>an aster</u>).

7. A plant that grows year after year is (an annual, <u>a perennial</u>).

Grow Your Own Garden

You Need

- 2 packages of seeds
- container with drainage holes
- potting soil
- plant dish or tray
- pencil
- graph paper

1. Start your own garden. The plants can be grown in the classroom or outdoors.

2. Choose containers to hold the soil. You can use plant pots (6-inch or larger) or make your own containers by carefully poking drainage holes in the bottom of large yogurt containers or half-gallon milk containers with the tops cut off.

3. Fill two containers with soil. Water lightly. Put a plant dish under each container to catch draining water.

4. Plant several seeds in each container. Read the directions on the package to see how deep the seeds should be planted. Keep the soil moist but not soggy.

5. Place the containers on a sunny windowsill. Check them each day. Observe the stages of plant growth. Record the growth on a graph.

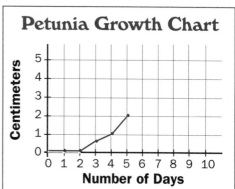

Petunia Growth Chart

Write the Answer

What do you think would happen if you put the containers with seeds in a dark closet? Explain your answer.

The seeds would not sprout.

If this happened

to seedlings, they would die.

Fill in the circle in front of the word or phrase that best completes each sentence. The first one is done for you.

1. Pollen is made in the top part of the
   - ⓐ pistils.
   - ● stamens.
   - ⓒ petals.

2. The female part of the flower is the
   - ⓐ pistil.
   - ⓑ sepal.
   - ⓒ stamen.

3. Plants that grow year after year are
   - ⓐ annuals.
   - ⓑ buds.
   - ⓒ perennials.

4. Moving pollen from a stamen to a pistil is called
   - ⓐ pollination.
   - ⓑ photosynthesis.
   - ⓒ exchange.

5. Trees and grasses are pollinated by
   - ⓐ bulbs.
   - ⓑ water.
   - ⓒ the wind.

6. Many orchids grow in climates that are
   - ⓐ hot and dry.
   - ⓑ hot and damp.
   - ⓒ cool and damp.

Fill in the missing words.

7. The male parts of a flower are _____stamens_____. (stamens, sepals)

8. Tulips grow from _____bulbs_____. (stems, bulbs)

9. Flower buds are protected by _____sepals_____. (leaves, sepals)

Write the answer on the lines.

10. Why are some insects attracted to flowers?

    _____Insects are attracted to flowers_____

    _____by the smell of the flowers_____

    _____and the bright colors of the petals._____

UNIT 3
Grasses and Cereals

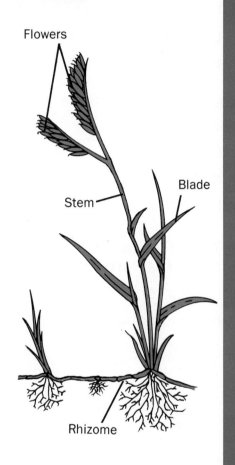

Flowers

Stem

Blade

Rhizome

Grasses

Grasses grow everywhere. They can be found in deserts and on snowy mountains. Some grow in water. Like other green plants, grasses have chlorophyll and make their own food.

Grass plants have spear-shaped leaves called **blades.** The blades grow from stems that are jointed. A blade grows from each joint on the stem. Grass stems grow fast.

There are thousands of grasses. Some are only 1 inch high. Others can be more than 100 feet high. Like most plants, grasses have roots that take in water and minerals from soil. These roots help hold soil and keep it from washing away.

Most grasses are either annuals or perennials. Annual grasses die at the end of the growing season. New seeds must be planted each year.

Perennial grasses live through the winter and grow again year after year. Some perennial grasses have stems called **rhizomes** that grow underground. Rhizomes spread out to start new grass plants.

Most grasses have tiny flowers. Each flower usually has both male and female parts, so the flowers can make fruits. The fruits of grasses are called **grains.**

Some grasses are cereal grasses. Their grains are used to make cereals and flour. Wheat, corn, rice, and oats are cereal grasses. Cereal grasses grow well in the part of the United States called the grasslands. Kansas and Nebraska are two states in the grassland area.

A. Fill in the missing words.

1. Grass plants have spear-shaped leaves called __blades__. (stems, blades)

2. New seeds must be planted each year for __annual grasses__ to grow. (annual grasses, perennial grasses)

3. Some perennial grasses have stems called __rhizomes__ that grow underground. (rhizomes, blades)

4. Most grasses have __tiny__ flowers. (tiny, huge)

5. The fruits of grass plants are called __grains__. (grains, blades)

6. Wheat, corn, rice, and oats are __cereal grasses__. (cereal grasses, stems)

7. Cereal grasses grow well in the part of the United States called the __grasslands__. (grasslands, desert)

B. Answer True or False.

1. All grasses are very short plants. __False__

2. The fruits of grasses are called grains. __True__

3. Rhizomes spread out to start new grass plants. __True__

4. The roots of grass plants do not help hold soil. __False__

5. Grasses make their own food. __True__

C. Answer the questions.

1. How do some perennial grasses spread out? __They have stems__ called rhizomes that grow underground. Rhizomes spread out to start new grass plants.

2. How do the roots of grasses protect the soil? __Roots__ help hold soil and keep it from washing away.

41

Lawn Grasses and Weeds

Lawn Grass

Dandelion

There are many kinds of **lawn grasses.** Most lawn grasses are perennials that grow year after year. These short grasses are used to cover ball fields, playgrounds, and yards.

Kentucky bluegrass is a lawn grass that will grow in most places. Other lawn grasses need a special climate or special soil. For example, Bermuda grass and St. Augustine grass need a warm, dry climate.

Most plants grow from their tips. Grass does not. It grows from the part of the stem closest to the ground. So cutting grasses does not harm the grass plants. In fact, cutting makes grass plants grow thicker.

Lawn grasses often have underground stems, or rhizomes. New plants grow along the rhizomes.

Insects and weeds are enemies of lawn grasses. Some insects lay eggs in grass. The eggs hatch into wormlike grubs. Grubs eat parts of the roots. Then grass cannot get the water and minerals it needs and it may die.

Weeds are plants that grow where they are not wanted. They crowd out other plants such as lawn grasses. Lawn grasses need water, sunlight, and minerals to make the food they need to grow. Weeds use up water and minerals in the soil.

Dandelions are weeds. Each dandelion flower makes many seeds that get scattered by the wind. The seeds fall to the ground and grow into new dandelions. It is very hard to get rid of dandelions.

A. Answer True or False.

1. Most lawn grasses are perennials. _____True_____

2. Grass grows from its tips. _____False_____

3. Cutting makes grass plants grow thicker. _____True_____

4. Lawn grasses often have underground stems. _____True_____

5. Insects and weeds are helpful to lawn grasses. _____False_____

B. Write helpful or harmful to show if each thing is helpful or harmful to lawn grasses.

1. weeds _____harmful_____

2. minerals _____helpful_____

3. sunlight _____helpful_____

4. grubs _____harmful_____

5. water _____helpful_____

C. Answer the questions.

1. What are weeds? _____Weeds are plants that grow where_____ _____they are not wanted._____

2. What happens to grass plants when they are cut? _____Cutting_____ _____makes grass plants grow thicker._____

3. How do some insects harm grass? _____Some insects lay eggs in_____ _____grass. The eggs hatch into wormlike grubs. Grubs eat_____ _____parts of the roots. Then grass cannot get the water_____ _____and minerals it needs and it may die._____

4. What are short grasses used to cover? _____Short grasses are_____ _____used to cover ball fields, playgrounds, and yards._____

Wheat

Wheat Grains

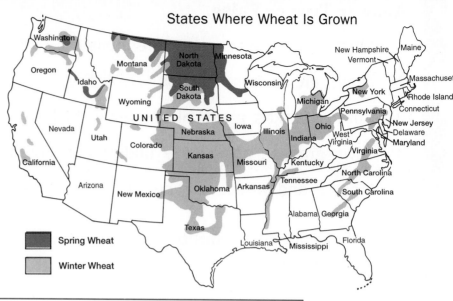

Wheat is a cereal grass. It is an annual, so it must be planted each year. Wheat is important because it is used by many people throughout the world for food.

There are many kinds of wheat. Winter wheat grows in mild climates. Spring wheat grows in places with very cold winters. Look at the map above. Do you live in a state where wheat is grown?

Winter wheat is planted in the fall. The roots stay alive through the winter. In the spring, wheat flowers develop. Later the grains form. Each wheat plant makes about 50 grains.

Some wheat grains are used to make cereals. But the most important product we get from wheat is flour. To make flour, wheat grains are crushed and ground into powder. When the whole grain is used, whole-wheat flour is made. Sometimes the outside of the grain is removed before the grains are crushed and ground. The outside of the grain is fed to animals. Then the grains are made into white flour. Both white and whole-wheat flour can be made into breads, cakes, cookies, pasta, and other foods.

Even wheat stems are useful. Dried wheat stems are called straw. Straw can be used as a fertilizer to improve soil. It can also be made into hats, baskets, and paper.

A. Fill in the missing words.

1. Wheat is a ___cereal___ grass. (cereal, weed)

2. Winter wheat is planted in the ___fall___. (winter, fall)

3. Wheat grains are crushed and ground to make ___flour___. (straw, flour)

4. The outside of wheat grains is fed to ___animals___. (people, animals)

5. Dried wheat stems are called ___straw___. (grains, straw)

6. Flour can be made into breads and ___pasta___. (pasta, straw)

B. Answer <u>True</u> or <u>False</u>.

1. Wheat grains are used to make cereals. ___True___

2. The outside of the grain is never used. ___False___

3. Winter wheat and spring wheat are two kinds of wheat. ___True___

4. Wheat grains can be made into whole-wheat or white flour.
   ___True___

5. The roots of winter wheat cannot stay alive through winter.
   ___False___

6. Straw can be made into hats, baskets, and paper. ___True___

C. Answer the questions.

1. Why is wheat important? ___It is used by many people___
   ___throughout the world for food.___

2. In which state is the most spring wheat grown? _____
   ___North Dakota___

3. What are wheat grains used for? ___Some wheat grains are___
   ___used to make cereals. The most important product___
   ___we get from wheat is flour.___

Corn

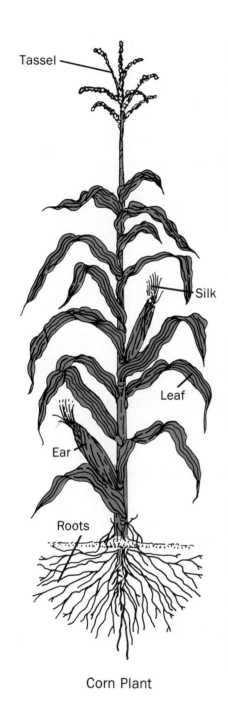

Tassel

Silk

Leaf

Ear

Roots

Corn Plant

Corn is another annual cereal grass that must be replanted each year. Its stem is not hollow like most grasses. But the stem is jointed like other grass plants. A leaf grows from each joint.

Corn plants have two kinds of flowers. The yellow <u>tassel</u> at the top of the plant has male flowers. Male flowers make pollen. The female flowers are found on the <u>ear</u> of the corn plant. The ear is a spike that grows from where a leaf joins a stem. Female flowers have long threadlike <u>silks</u> that catch pollen.

When the wind blows, pollen from male flowers may land on the silks. Then the ear is <u>fertilized</u> and the corn grains, or <u>kernels</u>, grow. Each kernel is a seed. There are many seeds on each ear.

Today, corn is our most important crop. The United States produces more corn than any other country. Corn is also important throughout the world because it has so many uses.

Corn needs rich soil to grow. This rich soil can be found in the midwestern part of the United States. It is called the Corn Belt. <u>Iowa</u>, <u>Illinois</u>, and <u>Nebraska</u> are three states in the Corn Belt.

There are hundreds of uses for corn. Its most important use is as a food for farm animals. People eat corn in many forms. We eat corn on the cob and popcorn. Corn is used to make cereals, cooking oil, and syrup. It can also be ground into cornmeal to make tortillas or cornbread. Corn is even used in making glue, soap, and alcohol.

A. **Use each word to write a sentence about corn.**

1. tassel _____ Sentences will vary. _____

   _____

2. kernel _____

   _____

3. Corn Belt _____

   _____

B. **Answer True or False.**

1. Corn is a cereal grass. _____True_____

2. Corn is an annual plant. _____True_____

3. The female part of the plant is the tassel. _____False_____

4. Each kernel of corn is a seed. _____True_____

5. Female flowers are found on the ear of corn. _____True_____

6. Today, corn is not an important crop in the United States.

   _____False_____

C. **Answer the questions.**

1. How does each ear of corn catch pollen? _____Female flowers_____

   _____have long threadlike silks that catch pollen._____

2. Where can the rich soil needed to grow corn be found? _____This_____

   _____rich soil can be found in the midwestern part of_____

   _____the United States. It is called the Corn Belt._____

3. What are three forms of corn that people eat? _____Answers will_____

   _____vary, but should include: corn on the cob, cereals,_____

   _____popcorn, cornbread, and tortillas._____

4. What is the most important use for corn? _____Its most important_____

   _____use is as food for farm animals._____

Rice

Rice Fields

Rice is a cereal grass. It is an annual and grows from seeds. Rice needs a lot of water and sunshine to grow. In fact, rice plants are grown in 4 to 8 inches of water. That is why rice can grow in places that are too warm and wet for other cereal grasses.

Rice is grown in many countries. China and India grow the most rice. In the United States, rice grows in Arkansas, California, Texas, and Louisiana.

How does rice get from the plant to your plate? First, rice grains are removed from the plant and sent to a mill. At the mill, the outer layer is taken off. Brown rice is still covered with a thin brown skin called bran. Because brown rice is rich in vitamins and minerals, it is good for people to eat. But brown rice spoils easily. So most brown rice is milled again. When the bran is removed, the rice is white. Both brown and white rice can be cooked and eaten.

Rice is the main food for many people, especially people living in Asia. Rice is used to make cereals. Rice grains can also be used to make glue, starch, and sugar. The stems of rice plants are made into rope, clothing, and paper.

A. Write the letter for the correct answer.

1. Rice grows where it is ____c____ .
    (a) cold and dry   (b) cold and wet   (c) warm and wet

2. Rice is grown from ____a____ .
    (a) seeds   (b) bulbs   (c) stems

3. Brown rice is covered with a brown skin called ____c____ .
    (a) wood   (b) grain   (c) bran

4. People can cook and eat ____c____ .
    (a) only brown rice   (b) only white rice
    (c) both brown and white rice

5. To remove the bran, brown rice is ____a____ .
    (a) milled again   (b) boiled again   (c) spoiled

B. Answer <u>True</u> or <u>False</u>.

1. Rice is grown only in the United States. __False__

2. Rice needs a lot of water and sunshine to grow. __True__

3. Brown rice is never used as food. __False__

4. Rice is used to make cereals. __True__

5. Rice is the main food for many people. __True__

6. Brown rice is rich in vitamins and minerals. __True__

7. Rice is a cereal grass. __True__

C. Answer the questions.

1. Which two countries grow the most rice? __China and__
    __India grow the most rice.__

2. Why is brown rice a good food for people to eat? __Brown__
    __rice is rich in vitamins and minerals.__

3. What are the stems of rice plants made into? __The stems__
    __of rice plants are made into rope, clothing,__
    __and paper.__

Oats

Oats

Oats are another kind of annual cereal grass. They grow best in a cool, moist climate that has very fertile soil. Russia grows more oats than any other country. In the United States, many oats are grown in the cool northern states of South Dakota and Minnesota.

Most oats are used as food for farm animals, especially horses. Some oats are grown for hay. Hay is harvested while the plants are still green and the grains are soft. Hay is used to feed farm animals in winter.

Oats are an important food because they are high in protein. They are also a good source of vitamins. The seeds from oat plants are used to make oatmeal and other cereals. Oat grains can also be ground into flour.

A. Answer True or False.

1. Oats are a kind of annual cereal grass. ___True___

2. Most oats are used as food for people. ___False___

3. Oats grow best in a cool, moist climate. ___True___

4. Seeds from oat plants are used to make cereals. ___True___

B. Answer the questions.

1. Which country grows more oats than any other country? _____
   Russia grows more oats than any other country.

2. Why are oats an important food? ___Oats are an important food because they are high in protein. They are also a good source of vitamins.___

50

Sugar Cane

Sugar cane is not a cereal grass. It is a perennial grass and can grow for many years. Most cereal grasses are annuals and grow from seeds. This is not true of sugar cane. To grow sugar cane, the stems are cut up and planted. New plants grow from each joint on the stem.

Sugar cane grows in warm climates that get a lot of rain. In the United States, Florida, Hawaii, and Louisiana grow sugar cane.

While cereal grass is grown for its grains, sugar cane is grown for its stems. The stems are made into sugar, syrup, and molasses. First, the leaves are removed from the stems. Next, the stems are cut and sent to a mill. There they are crushed to squeeze out their sugary juice. After the juice goes through many more steps, white sugar is made.

Sugar Cane

A. **Answer True or False.**

1. Sugar cane is not a cereal grass. _____True_____

2. New sugar cane plants grow from seeds. _____False_____

3. Sugar cane grows in a cold climate. _____False_____

B. **The steps below describe how sugar is made from sugar cane. Number the steps in the correct order. The first one is done for you.**

___4___ After the juice goes through many more steps, white sugar is made.

___1___ First, the leaves are removed from the stems.

___3___ There they are crushed to squeeze out their sugary juice.

___2___ Next, the stems are cut and sent to a mill.

Bamboo

Bamboo

Bamboo is a giant perennial grass that lives for many years. It has hollow, woody stems that are jointed. Bamboo stems are stronger than other grass stems. Layers of bamboo stems are almost as strong as steel.

Long, narrow leaves grow from the joints of the bamboo plant. New plants grow around the base of old plants. New bamboo shoots grow quickly along rhizomes, or underground stems. One bamboo grew 3 feet in one day! Some may grow to be 120 feet tall.

Bamboo has flowers like other grasses, but they may bloom only once in 30 years. Certain kinds of bamboo flower only once every 100 years. Yet when they do, plants of that kind of bamboo all over the world bloom at the same time.

Bamboo needs a warm, wet climate. Many kinds grow in Asia. In Asia, bamboo has more uses than any other plant. It is used to make entire houses, furniture, fences, baskets, rope, and paper.

Fill in the missing words.

1. Bamboo is a giant _____perennial grass_____.
   (perennial grass, annual grass)

2. Bamboo stems are _____stronger_____ than other grass stems.
   (stronger, weaker)

3. Bamboo has hollow ___woody___ stems. (soft, woody)

4. New bamboo shoots grow _____quickly_____ along rhizomes, or underground stems. (slowly, quickly)

5. Bamboo needs a warm, ___wet___ climate. (wet, dry)

Use the words below to complete the sentences.

Annual	Corn Belt	rhizomes
bamboo	grains	spring
blades	grass	sugar cane
bran	kernel	weeds
cereal	lawn grass	wheat
corn	oats	

1. Grass plants have leaves called _____blades_____.

2. Insects and _____weeds_____ are enemies of lawn grasses.

3. The fruits of grasses are called _____grains_____.

4. White flour is made from the cereal grass called _____wheat_____.

5. Tassels and silks are part of a _____corn_____ plant.

6. Each grain of corn is called a _____kernel_____.

7. Rice is a _____cereal_____ grass.

8. Some perennial grasses have underground stems called _____rhizomes_____.

9. The thin, brown skin of a rice grain is called _____bran_____.

10. A grass used to make entire houses, furniture, and fences is _____bamboo_____.

11. A cereal grain high in protein and vitamins is _____oats_____.

12. A perennial grass grown to make sugar is _____sugar cane_____.

13. Two kinds of wheat are winter wheat and _____spring_____ wheat.

14. Rich soil to grow corn can be found in the _____Corn Belt_____.

15. _____Annual_____ grasses die at the end of the growing season.

16. Kentucky bluegrass is a _____lawn grass_____ that will grow in most places.

Compare the Nutrition of Cereal Grains

You Need

- **Nutrition Facts label**
- **pencil**
- **large sheet of paper**

1. Corn, rice, oat, and wheat grains are often used to make cereal. Which grain do you think is the most nutritious? Write your guess in the space provided.

2. You can find the answer to this question by comparing the labels on different kinds of cereals. Look at the diagram. It compares the nutrition of corn cereal with wheat cereal.

3. On a large sheet of paper, make a chart like the one in the diagram.

4. Bring in a *Nutrition Facts* label from an empty box of cereal. Use this label to fill in the third column of your chart.

5. The most nutritious cereal will be high in protein, carbohydrates, and fiber. It will be low in calories, fat, and sugar. Circle the column of the most nutritious cereal on your chart. Compare your findings with those of other students.

Most Nutritious: _____

Nutrition Facts for 1 Serving	Corn	Wheat	
Calories	110	190	
Fat (grams)	0 g	1 g	
Total Carbohydrate (grams)	26 g	41 g	
Dietary Fiber (grams)	0 g	5 g	
Sugars (grams)	3 g	5 g	
Protein (grams)	2 g	5 g	

Write the Answer

Name your favorite cereal and explain whether you think it would score high or low in nutrition.

Students should state their favorite cereal and try to identify

the cereal grain used to produce it. If students choose a cereal

with a high sugar content, they may score it low in nutrition.

UNIT 3 Test

Fill in the circle in front of the word or phrase that best completes each sentence. The first one is done for you.

1. The spear-shaped leaves of grass plants are called
   - (a) grains.
   - ● blades.
   - (c) tassels.

2. A lawn grass that will grow in most places is
   - (a) bamboo.
   - (b) sugar cane.
   - (c) Kentucky bluegrass.

3. Brown rice has a thin skin called
   - (a) wheat.
   - (b) bran.
   - (c) grain.

4. Grass stems that grow underground are called
   - (a) joints.
   - (b) leaves.
   - (c) rhizomes.

5. The most important crop in the United States is
   - (a) corn.
   - (b) rice.
   - (c) lawn grass.

6. Some oats are grown for
   - (a) wheat.
   - (b) their roots.
   - (c) hay.

Fill in the missing words.

7. White flour is made from _____wheat grains_____.
   (wheat grains, oat stems)

8. Sugar is made from the stems of _____sugar cane_____.
   (wheat, sugar cane)

9. A giant grass is _____bamboo_____. (bamboo, rice)

Write the answer on the lines.

10. What is the climate like in which oats grow best?

    Oats grow best in a cool, moist climate.

55

The Parts of a Tree

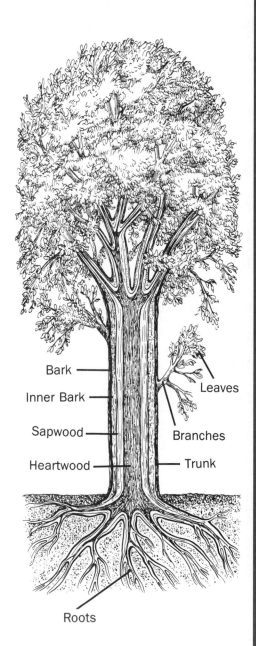

Bark

Inner Bark

Sapwood

Heartwood

Leaves

Branches

Trunk

Roots

In most ways, trees are like all other green plants. Like other plants, trees have roots, stems, and leaves. But trees are much larger than other plants. Most trees grow 15 to 20 feet tall. There are even trees as tall as 30-story buildings.

A tree's roots take in water and minerals from the soil. Roots also help hold a tree in place. Some trees have one main root called a **taproot**. The taproot grows straight down in the soil. Other trees have **fibrous roots**. Fibrous roots are a system of roots that spread out in the soil.

The hard, woody stem of a tree is called a **trunk**. The trunk is made up of several layers. There is a tough outside layer called **bark**. Bark protects the tree against insects and diseases. It also protects a tree from too much heat or cold. Under the bark is **sapwood**. Sapwood is full of tubes that carry water and minerals from the roots of the tree to the leaves. This mixture of water and minerals is called **sap**.

Between the sapwood and the bark is the **inner bark**. Food that is made in the leaves is carried to other parts of the tree through the inner bark. The center of the trunk is **heartwood**, the oldest, darkest, and hardest wood in the tree. The heartwood helps support the tree.

The leaves of a tree grow from the branches. The branches hold the leaves up to the light. In sunlight, leaves make all of the food for the tree.

A. **Answer True or False.**

1. Trees have roots, stems, and leaves. ___True___

2. Bark protects a tree against insects and disease. ___True___

3. A tree trunk is a soft stem. ___False___

4. Sapwood is full of tubes. ___True___

5. Heartwood is the tree's soft, new wood. ___False___

6. Roots help hold a tree in place. ___True___

B. **Use each word to write a sentence about trees.**

1. trunk _____ Sentences will vary. _____

_____

2. bark _____

_____

3. leaves _____

_____

C. **Underline the correct words.**

1. The stem of a tree is called the (sap, branch, <u>trunk</u>).

2. Tubes that carry water are in the (<u>sapwood</u>, heartwood).

3. (<u>Leaves</u>, Roots, Trunks) make all of the food for a tree.

4. Fibrous roots (grow straight down, <u>spread out</u>).

D. **Answer the questions.**

1. What is the job of the leaves of a tree? ___In sunlight, the___

__leaves make all of the food for a tree.__

2. What carries water and minerals from the roots of a tree to its leaves?

__Sapwood is full of tubes that carry water and__

__minerals from the roots to the leaves.__

How a Tree Grows

Tree Growth Ring

Tree Began to Grow
Years With a Little Rain
Years With a Lot of Rain

How Bark Patterns Are Formed

The Old Bark Splits
and New Bark Forms Underneath

Different Kinds of Bark

Smooth	Shaggy	Papery

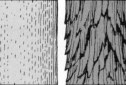

American Beech	Shagbark Hickory	Paper Birch

Trees are the oldest living things on Earth. There are trees in the United States that have lived more than 4,000 years.

Trees are always growing. The branches of a tree grow out from their tips. This growth makes the branches longer. The trunk of a tree grows from its tip and gets taller. The tips of the branches and the trunk continue to grow as long as a tree is alive.

The trunk of a tree also grows thicker as new wood is made under the bark. The wood is made of tubes that form in a circle called a **growth ring**. In most trees, a new growth ring forms every year. You may have seen growth rings in the trunks of trees that have been cut down. You can tell how old a tree is by counting the growth rings.

Not all growth rings are the same. Some rings are thicker than others. Thick rings form in years when there is a lot of rain. Thin rings form in years when there is little rain.

Different kinds of trees have different kinds of bark. The kind of bark is one way to identify trees. As the trunk of a tree grows and gets thicker, the bark might crack. These cracks form a pattern in the bark. Each kind of tree has a different pattern. Look at the patterns of tree bark shown in the drawing.

The roots of a tree also grow out from their tips. This makes the roots longer. As they get longer, roots also get thicker. Have you ever seen a sidewalk pushed up by the root of a tree?

A. Answer True or False.

1. Trees are the oldest living things on Earth. ___True___

2. Trees are always growing. ___True___

3. Trees grow taller but not thicker. ___False___

4. New wood is made under the bark of a tree. ___True___

5. All growth rings are the same. ___False___

6. All tree bark looks the same. ___False___

7. The roots of a tree grow out from the tips. ___True___

B. Fill in the missing words.

1. The branches of a tree grow out from their ___tips___. (rings, tips)

2. Different kinds of trees have different kinds of ___bark___. (bark, soil)

3. New wood is made under the ___bark___. (bark, roots)

4. In most trees, a new growth ring forms every ___year___. (day, year)

5. Thick growth rings form in years when there is a lot of ___rain___. (sunlight, rain)

6. As roots get ___longer___, they also get thicker. (longer, shorter)

C. Answer the questions.

1. How do tree branches grow longer? ___The branches of a tree grow out from their tips. This makes the branches longer.___

2. What can you tell about a tree by counting its growth rings? ___You can tell how old a tree is by counting the growth rings.___

Evergreen Trees

Fir Tree

All trees lose their leaves. A maple tree loses all its leaves each fall. But some trees, such as pines and live oaks, stay green all year long. These trees are called **evergreens**. Many evergreens grow new leaves before the old leaves fall off. Other evergreens keep their leaves for several years.

Many evergreens have leaves shaped like needles. Most evergreens with needlelike leaves make cones. Trees that make cones are called **conifers**. The seeds of conifers are made in cones.

Pine trees are conifers. Pines have long, needlelike leaves that grow in bunches. Pines can grow in cold places. They can grow in sandy or rocky soil. Pines grow very fast, and most have trunks that grow tall and straight. For these reasons, pine trees are often used as wood.

Spruce and fir trees are conifers, too. These trees have cones and needlelike leaves. The beautiful silvery blue spruce is often planted in gardens. You can recognize fir trees by their cones. They grow straight up from the branches. Some firs are sources of wood. Others, like the balsam fir, are often used as Christmas trees. Balsam needles have a pleasant smell.

The live oak is an evergreen that does not have cones or needlelike leaves. Its leaves are wide and fat. Live oaks grow in warm climates. They are found along the coast in the southern United States and in areas of the Southwest.

A. **Underline the correct words.**

1. All trees lose their (cones, <u>leaves</u>).

2. The seeds of conifers are made in (needles, <u>cones</u>).

3. Pine trees and live oaks are called (<u>evergreens</u>, cones).

4. (All, <u>Some</u>) evergreens keep their leaves for several years.

5. Live oaks grow in (<u>warm</u>, cold) climates.

B. **Answer <u>True</u> or <u>False</u>.**

1. Spruce and fir trees are conifers. _____True_____

2. The seeds of conifers are made in the leaves. _____False_____

3. The live oak is an evergreen. _____True_____

4. All evergreens have wide, flat leaves. _____False_____

5. Pine trees grow very fast. _____True_____

C. **Write <u>pine</u>, <u>live oak</u>, or <u>both</u> after each description.**

1. has wide, flat leaves _____live oak_____

2. is a conifer _____pine_____

3. is found along the coast in the southern United States

   _____live oak_____

4. can grow in cold places _____pine_____

5. an evergreen _____both_____

6. has needlelike leaves _____pine_____

D. **Answer the questions.**

1. What are evergreens? _____Evergreens are trees that stay_____

   _____green all year long._____

2. What are conifers? _____Trees that make cones are_____

   _____called conifers._____

Deciduous Trees

Spring   Summer   Fall   Winter

Trees that lose all their leaves at a certain time each year are called **deciduous** trees. Birch, beech, hickory, oak, and maple are deciduous trees. These trees have broad, flat leaves. In the northern United States, deciduous trees usually lose their leaves in the fall. New leaves grow in the spring. In the south, where it is warmer, deciduous trees keep their leaves longer. They also grow new leaves earlier.

Deciduous trees change from season to season. In summer, they are covered with green leaves. The green leaves make food all summer. The trees use the food to grow. In the fall, the leaves of northern deciduous trees like maples and oaks turn red, yellow, or orange. Later, the leaves die, turn brown, and fall to the ground. Before losing their leaves, the trees store food made by the leaves. The branches of the trees store the food until spring. All winter the branches are bare, and the tree rests. It lives on its stored food.

In spring, the tree uses stored food to grow new leaves and flowers. The seeds that make new trees form in the flowers. By summer, green leaves cover the branches again. A year has passed.

A. Answer True or False.

1. In winter, a deciduous tree lives on its stored food. _____True_____

2. Deciduous trees are found only in the northern United States. _____False_____

3. Maple trees are deciduous. _____True_____

4. The leaves of northern deciduous trees change color in the fall. _____True_____

5. Deciduous trees change from season to season. _____True_____

B. Fill in the missing words.

1. Deciduous trees lose all their leaves at a certain time each _____year_____. (day, year)

2. All winter the branches of a deciduous tree are _____bare_____. (bare, covered with leaves)

3. In _____summer_____, deciduous trees are covered with green leaves. (winter, summer)

4. In the winter, a deciduous tree _____rests_____. (rests, makes food)

5. In _____spring_____, a deciduous tree uses stored food to grow new leaves and flowers. (winter, spring)

C. Answer the questions.

1. Where are the seeds that make new deciduous trees formed? _The seeds that make new trees form in the flowers._

2. What do deciduous trees do before losing their leaves? _The trees store food made by the leaves._

3. How does a deciduous tree live through the winter? _The tree lives on its stored food._

63

Deciduous Forests

Deciduous Forest

A **forest** is a place where many trees grow. But smaller plants and a variety of animals are also found in a forest.

A forest is made up of several layers. The tallest trees form the top layer, called the **canopy**. The canopy gets most of the sunlight in the forest. The leaves in the canopy make the most food in the forest. The tops of shorter trees form a middle layer called the **understory**. Smaller plants, such as shrubs, wildflowers, grasses, and mosses, grow on the bottom layer near the forest floor.

The kinds of trees, plants, and animals that live in a forest depend on the soil and climate. **Deciduous forests** contain mostly deciduous trees. They grow best where there is some rain all through the year. Such areas often have cold winters and warm summers.

Deciduous forests are found in the eastern United States, most of central Europe, and part of eastern Asia. The trees of the canopy of deciduous forests may grow to be 100 feet tall.

More small plants can grow beneath the canopy in the early spring. Because the deciduous trees still have no leaves, these small plants get the sunlight they need. By summer, new leaves grow on the trees. Then only plants that can live in shade grow on the forest floor.

Many different kinds of animals live in the deciduous forest. Squirrels move through the canopy. Deer feed on plants near the forest floor. Thousands of birds nest in the forest.

A. Answer True or False.

1. A forest is a place where few trees grow. _____False_____

2. A forest is made up of several layers. _____True_____

3. Shrubs and wildflowers grow below the understory. _____True_____

4. Birds are never found in deciduous forests. _____False_____

5. Deciduous forests grow best in hot, dry climates. _____False_____

B. Write the letter for the correct answer.

1. The tallest trees form a layer called the ____a____ .
   (a) canopy   (b) floor   (c) understory

2. Trees in the canopy get most of the ____c____ .
   (a) water   (b) soil   (c) sunlight

3. The kinds of trees, plants, and animals that live in a forest depend on

   the ____c____ .
   (a) soil   (b) climate   (c) both a and b

C. Fill in the missing words.

1. Deciduous forests grow where there is some ____rain____ all through
   the year. (rain, snow)

2. Trees of the canopy layer may grow to be ____100____ feet tall.
   (10, 100)

3. The tops of shorter trees form a layer called the ____understory____ .
   (understory, canopy)

4. In the spring, small forest plants can get the ____sunlight____ they
   need. (shade, sunlight)

D. Answer the question.

Why can more small plants grow beneath the canopy in the early spring?

_____Because the deciduous trees still have no_____

_____leaves, these small plants get the sunlight_____

_____they need._____

65

Coniferous Forests

Coniferous Forest

Remember that coniferous trees make seeds in cones. Most conifers are evergreens. Many evergreens have leaves shaped like needles.

Coniferous forests usually grow in cold climates. Many are found across northern Europe, Asia, and North America. Spruce, fir, and pine trees make up the canopy of these forests. These trees can grow to be about 75 feet tall.

Coniferous forests are also found on the West Coast of the United States. There the climate is warm and wet. Huge redwoods and giant sequoia trees grow in these forests.

It is dark in a coniferous forest. The conifers, which are covered with needles all year long, keep sunlight from reaching the forest floor. Only plants that need little sun can grow under these trees. The forest floor and the trunks of many trees are often covered with moss. A layer of fallen needles also covers the forest floor.

Bears, wolves, moose, and snowshoe rabbits are just some of the animals that live in coniferous forests. Also, birds such as owls and woodpeckers make their homes there.

A. Answer True or False.

1. Most conifers are evergreens. _____True_____

2. Spruce trees grow in deciduous forests. _____False_____

3. Trees in a coniferous forest can grow to be 75 feet tall. _____True_____

4. Coniferous forests usually grow in cold climates. _____True_____

5. Plants that need a lot of sunlight grow on the forest floor.
   _____False_____

6. Moose and bear may be found in a coniferous forest. _____True_____

B. Write the letter for the correct answer.

1. Many evergreens have leaves shaped like _____c_____ .
   (a) hands   (b) triangles   (c) needles

2. Coniferous forests can grow in _____a_____ climates.
   (a) cold   (b) hot   (c) desert

3. Spruce, fir, and _____a_____ trees are conifers.
   (a) pine   (b) palm   (c) maple

4. In a coniferous forest, the forest floor and the trunks of many trees
   are often covered with _____b_____ .
   (a) flowers   (b) moss   (c) shrubs

5. Redwoods and giant sequoias grow where the climate is _____c_____ .
   (a) warm   (b) wet   (c) both warm and wet

6. Coniferous trees make seeds in _____c_____ .
   (a) roots   (b) trunks   (c) cones

C. Answer the question.

Why can plants that need only a little sun grow under the trees in a coniferous

forest? _____ The conifers, which are covered with _____

_____ needles all year long, keep sunlight from reaching _____

_____ the forest floor. _____

Tropical Rain Forests

Tropical Rain Forest

Tropical rain forests are found near the equator where the weather is hot and wet all year round. More than 100 inches of rain may fall in a tropical rain forest each year.

The world's largest tropical rain forest surrounds the Amazon River in South America. This rain forest is the size of the United States. Rain forests are also found in areas of Central America, Africa, Asia, and on islands like Puerto Rico and Hawaii.

There are more kinds of plants and animals in tropical rain forests than anywhere else on Earth. Most of the plants are flowering trees. Some of the trees found in the tropical rain forest are ebony, teak, rosewood, and mahogany. In the hot, rainy forest, the trees grow quickly. The taller trees form a canopy of leaves more than 120 feet above the forest floor. Some huge trees may even grow to be 200 feet high!

In a rain forest, the trees block sunlight from the forest floor. Only a few kinds of plants can grow in the darkness under the trees. But many kinds of vines grow up along the trunks of the trees. Orchids may grow on the highest tree branches where there is more sunlight.

Most of the animals in a tropical rain forest live in the canopy where the food supply is greatest. Thousands of kinds of insects live in rain forests. A variety of birds, monkeys, and reptiles make their homes in rain forests, too.

A. Answer True or False.

1. Tropical rain forests are found where it is cool and dry. __False__

2. Only a few kinds of plants can grow under the trees. __True__

3. The trees in the hot, rainy forest grow slowly. __False__

4. Orchids may grow on the highest tree branches. __True__

5. The forest floor gets lots of sunlight. __False__

6. More kinds of plants and animals live in tropical rain forests than anywhere else on Earth. __True__

B. Fill in the missing words.

1. Most of the plants in a tropical rain forest are __flowering trees__. (flowering trees, pines)

2. In a rain forest, the trees block __sunlight__ from the forest floor. (insects, sunlight)

3. __Vines__ grow up along the trunks of the trees. (Vines, Mahogany)

4. A tree that is found in the tropical rain forest is __ebony__. (ebony, sequoia)

5. Most animals in a rain forest live __in the canopy__. (in the canopy, on the ground)

6. More than __100__ inches of rain may fall in a tropical rain forest each year. (100, 1,000)

C. Answer the questions.

1. What is the weather like in a tropical rain forest? __The weather is hot and wet all year round.__

2. Where do most of the animals in a tropical rain forest live?
   __Most of the animals in a tropical rain forest live in the canopy where the food supply is greatest.__

Maple Trees

Sugar Maple Tree

Maple Leaf

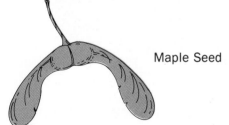
Maple Seed

There are more than 100 kinds of maple trees. Many maple trees grow in places that have cold winters and warm summers.

Maple trees are deciduous. They have broad, flat leaves shaped like hands. In the fall, the leaves usually turn red, orange, or yellow. During the winter, the trees are bare.

Maple trees make flowers in the spring. Then they make seeds. Two seeds grow together with a thin, flat wing on each side of the seeds. The wings help the seeds float on the wind. The wind can carry maple seeds far from the tree. When the seeds land on soil, they can grow into new trees.

People use maple trees in many ways. The sugar maple is the most useful tree. Its beautiful, strong wood is used to make furniture and floors. The sweet sap of the sugar maple is used to make maple syrup. The sap is collected in early spring. It takes about 40 gallons of sap to make 1 gallon of maple syrup.

A. Answer True or False.

1. Maple trees are deciduous. _____True_____

2. Maple trees always grow in places that are hot all year. _____False_____

B. Answer the question.

What is the sugar maple tree used for? _____Its wood is used to_____ make furniture and floors. The sap is used to make maple syrup.

Oak Trees

There are many kinds of oak trees. Deciduous oak trees grow where winters are cold. These oaks grow tall and wide. Many live for more than 200 years.

Deciduous oak trees change with the seasons. In the fall, their leaves turn red or brown. By spring, the old leaves have fallen off and new leaves have begun to grow.

Oak trees make male and female flowers in spring. The male flowers make pollen, which is carried by the wind to female flowers. When a female flower is pollinated, it forms an acorn. An acorn holds the seed that can grow into a new oak tree.

Evergreen oak trees grow where the weather is warm most of the year. One kind of evergreen oak tree is called the live oak. The live oak grows in the southern part of the United States. It has many branches that spread out far from the tree. Live oaks can live for hundreds of years.

Live Oak

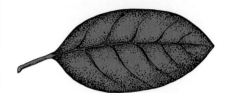

Live Oak Leaf

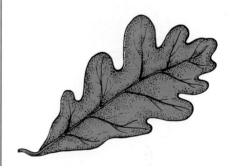

Deciduous Oak Leaf

A. **Answer True or False.**

1. All oaks are evergreens. __False__

2. Oak trees live only a few years. __False__

B. **Fill in the missing words.**

1. One kind of __evergreen__ oak tree is called the live oak. (evergreen, deciduous)

2. Evergreen oaks grow where the weather is __warm__ most of the year. (warm, cold)

71

Palm Trees

Cabbage Palm

Feather-Shaped

Fan-Shaped

There are about 2,600 kinds of palm plants. Some are vines and others are bushes. But most palms are trees. Palm trees grow in warm climates.

Palm trees can grow 100 feet tall. Most palm trees have just one stem, or trunk, and no branches. Their leaves, which stay green all year, grow out of the top of the trunk.

There are two main kinds of palm leaves. One kind has the shape of a feather and can grow 20 feet long. The second kind is shaped like a fan. These leaves may grow about 3 feet wide.

The cabbage palm has fan-shaped leaves. When the leaves are small, they form a bud at the top of the trunk. This bud, which tastes like cabbage, is eaten as a vegetable in some tropical countries.

Coconut palms usually grow near the ocean. They have leaves shaped like feathers. The fruits of this palm are the hard-shelled coconuts that grow in bunches under the leaves. Although they feel heavy, coconuts can float in water. They are often carried great distances in the ocean. Some coconuts then wash up on beaches and begin to grow new trees.

You may have eaten another fruit that comes from a palm tree. The fruit is called a date, and it comes from the date palm. While the coconut is a hard fruit, the date is soft with a hard seed at the center. Like coconuts, dates are often used in baked goods. The feather-shaped leaves of date palms are made into baskets and bags.

A. **Answer True or False.**

1. Most palms are trees. _____True_____

2. Palm trees have many branches. _____False_____

3. Palm trees grow in cold climates. _____False_____

4. Palm leaves are green all year. _____True_____

5. Most palm leaves are shaped like needles. _____False_____

6. Some palm trees have leaves shaped like feathers. _____True_____

7. Palm trees can grow 100 feet tall. _____True_____

B. **Use the words below to complete the sentences.**

date	ocean	trunk
fans	trees	warm

1. Palm plants can be vines, bushes, or _____trees_____.

2. Most palm trees have one stem, or _____trunk_____.

3. Palm leaves are shaped like feathers or _____fans_____.

4. Coconut palms usually grow near the _____ocean_____.

5. Palm trees grow where the climate is _____warm_____.

6. A palm fruit that is very soft is the _____date_____.

C. **Write coconut palm, cabbage palm, or date palm after each phrase.**

1. has fruits that wash up on beaches and grow new trees
   _____coconut palm_____

2. has soft fruit with a hard seed in the center _____date palm_____

3. has buds that can be eaten _____cabbage palm_____

4. has a fruit that can float in water _____coconut palm_____

5. has leaves shaped like fans _____cabbage palm_____

Sequoia Trees

Giant Sequoia

Sequoias are evergreen trees. They are the tallest trees on Earth. They are also some of the oldest. There are two kinds of sequoias. One is the redwood. The other is called the giant sequoia. The name "sequoia" comes from a Native American word for a big tree.

Redwoods grow in forests on the West Coast of the United States. These trees grow well in areas with warm, moist winters and cool, dry summers. Redwoods grow slowly, but they usually grow to between 200 and 275 feet high. The trunks of some redwoods can be more than 10 feet across. The leaves of redwoods are shaped like needles. The seeds are made in very small cones on the branches.

Giant sequoias grow in the same climate as redwoods. They are not as tall as redwoods, but their trunks are much larger. Giant sequoias also have leaves shaped like needles. Their cones are only about 2 inches long. Each small cone makes many seeds.

The largest tree in the world is a giant sequoia. The tree is known as the General Sherman. It is more than 270 feet tall. Its trunk is more than 30 feet wide. Some people think that the General Sherman tree is about 3,500 years old.

The General Sherman sequoia is in the Sequoia National Park in California. Sequoias are protected by law. People are not allowed to injure these trees or cut them down.

A. Fill in the missing words.

1. Sequoias are the _____tallest_____ trees on Earth. (shortest, tallest)

2. One kind of sequoia is a _____redwood____ tree. (redwood, maple)

3. Sequoias make seed in ____cones_____. (cones, needles)

4. The leaves of the sequoias are shaped like ____needles____. (cones, needles)

5. Redwoods grow in areas with warm, moist winters and cool, ____dry____ summers. (rainy, dry)

B. Answer True or False.

1. Sequoias are evergreen trees. ____True____

2. There are two kinds of sequoias. ____True____

3. Sequoias have leaves shaped like needles. ____True____

4. Giant sequoias are taller than redwoods, but their trunks are much smaller. ____False____

5. Redwoods grow very quickly. ____False____

6. Giant sequoias have cones that are more than 2 feet long. ____False____

7. Redwoods usually grow to be more than 200 feet tall. ____True____

C. Answer the questions.

1. What are the two kinds of sequoias? ____One is the redwood.____ ____The other is called the giant sequoia.____

2. Where do redwoods grow well? ____These trees grow well in____ ____areas with warm, moist winters and cool, dry summers.____

3. How do laws protect the sequoias? ____People are not allowed____ ____to injure these trees or cut them down.____

Magnolia Trees

Magnolia Tree

Magnolia Flower

Magnolias are flowering trees that grow in North America and Asia. Magnolia trees that grow in the southern United States are large evergreen trees. In the North, magnolias are smaller and deciduous. Remember that deciduous trees lose all their leaves at a certain time each year.

Magnolias grow from seeds. They grow so slowly that it may take some magnolias 20 years to form flowers. Most magnolias have sweet-smelling white flowers. The flowers are about 3 inches wide. Each flower has from 6 to 12 petals.

Magnolia leaves are oval shaped and can be from 3 to 6 inches long. One kind of magnolia has much larger leaves. It is called the big-leaf magnolia. Its leaves can be 30 inches long. The flowers of the big-leaf magnolia are the largest of any tree <u>native</u> to the United States. They can grow to be 10 inches across.

A. Answer <u>True</u> or <u>False</u>.

1. Magnolia trees make flowers. ___True___

2. Magnolia trees grow only in the southern part of the United States. ___False___

3. Magnolias grow from seeds. ___True___

B. Answer the question.

How are the magnolia trees in the southern United States different from those in the North? ___Magnolia trees in the southern United States are large evergreen trees. In the North, magnolias are smaller and deciduous.___

Part A

Read each sentence. Write <u>True</u> if the sentence is true. Write <u>False</u> if the sentence is false.

1. Trees have roots, stems, and leaves. ___True___

2. As a tree grows, it gets taller and thicker. ___True___

3. Bark protects a tree against insects and disease. ___True___

4. Evergreen trees drop all their leaves each fall. ___False___

5. A forest is a place where many trees grow. ___True___

6. Trees are the youngest living things on Earth. ___False___

Part B

Fill in the missing words.

1. The ___roots___ of a tree take in water and minerals from the soil. (roots, stems)

2. The ___leaves___ make food for a tree. (roots, leaves)

3. A tree that loses all its leaves each fall is ___deciduous___. (deciduous, evergreen)

4. A tree that makes seeds in cones is a ___conifer___. (conifer, palm)

5. In a deciduous forest, you might see a ___maple___ tree. (palm, maple)

6. ___Tropical rain___ forests grow where it is hot and wet all year round. (Tropical rain, Deciduous)

7. ___Palm___ trees have leaves shaped like feathers or fans. (Palm, Magnolia)

8. The tallest trees on Earth are the ___sequoias___. (oaks, sequoias)

9. ___Magnolia___ trees are evergreens in the southern United States and are deciduous in the North. (Magnolia, Sequoia)

10. Some ___evergreen___ trees have leaves shaped like needles. (evergreen, deciduous)

Adopt a Tree

You Need

- drawing paper
- writing paper
- tracing paper
- measuring tape
- pencils and crayons
- tree guides or encyclopedia
- tape

1. Find a nearby tree to adopt and study. Make a careful drawing of the tree. Label its parts.

2. Use a tree book or an encyclopedia to identify your tree. Find out if it is deciduous or evergreen.

3. Measure around the widest part of the trunk. How big is it? About how tall is the tree? How old do you think it is?

4. Make bark and leaf rubbings. Place tracing paper against the tree's bark or the underside of a leaf. Rub lightly with the flat side of a crayon to see a print.

5. Write a description of the tree and its surroundings. Where is it growing? Is it growing in full sun or shade? Tape the description to the bottom of your drawing and display it in the classroom.

My tree is a maple tree. It is growing in full sun on the street in front of my house. It is a deciduous tree. It loses all its leaves every fall.

Write the Answer

What three words would you use to describe your tree?

Answers will vary.

Students may use words such as large,

rough, hard, rustling, graceful, shady, or beautiful.

Fill in the circle in front of the word or phrase that best completes each sentence. The first one is done for you.

1. Tree roots that branch out are called
   - ● fibrous roots.
   - ⓑ taproots.
   - ⓒ trunks.

2. The trunk of a tree is made up of several
   - ⓐ leaves.
   - ⓑ branches.
   - Ⓒ layers.

3. Most evergreen trees are
   - ⓐ palms.
   - Ⓑ conifers.
   - ⓒ deciduous.

4. In the winter a deciduous tree
   - ⓐ makes flowers.
   - ⓑ makes leaves.
   - Ⓒ rests.

5. A tree that grows in a deciduous forest is a
   - ⓐ redwood.
   - ⓑ palm tree.
   - Ⓒ sugar maple.

6. One kind of sequoia is the
   - Ⓐ redwood.
   - ⓑ pine tree.
   - ⓒ spruce tree.

Fill in the missing words.

7. The branches of a tree grow out from their _____tips_____. (tips, centers)

8. Food for a tree is made in the _____leaves_____ of the tree. (roots, leaves)

9. Oak trees grow from _____acorns_____. (cones, acorns)

Write the answer on the lines.

10. Why do trees in a tropical rain forest grow quickly?

   The weather in a tropical rain forest is hot and wet.

   This makes the trees grow quickly.

Food from Green Plants

People eat many different kinds of plants.

You know that plants make their own food. People eat the parts of plants where food is stored. For example, people eat leaves, roots, stems, seeds, fruits, and even some flowers.

The food that plants make is a kind of sugar. Plants use some of this sugar to grow. They also change some sugar into starch. The starch is stored in the plants until it is needed. Plants also use sugar to make fats, proteins, and vitamins. All these substances are an important part of a healthy diet.

Sugars and starches are **carbohydrates.** Carbohydrates help your body produce energy. Fats also give your body energy. But for a healthy diet, you should not eat more fats than you need. Proteins help your body grow. Your body uses proteins to repair body tissue. The vitamins in plant foods help other substances in your body to do their job.

Answer True or False.

1. People eat the parts of plants where food is stored. __True__

2. Sugars and starches are proteins. __False__

3. Carbohydrates and fats help your body produce energy. __True__

Leaves

The green leaves of vegetables have many vitamins. Vitamins help your body use carbohydrates and fats for energy. They help build new cells. Vitamins help to keep you healthy.

One green leafy vegetable is cabbage. Cabbage has many thick leaves attached to a short stem. The cabbage plant stores food in these leaves. You can eat cabbage cooked or raw.

Spinach is another kind of leaf that is used as food. Spinach leaves can be cooked or eaten raw in a salad. Leaves from different kinds of lettuce can also be used in salads.

Some leaves are used to flavor foods. Have you ever eaten spaghetti with tomato sauce? The sauce may have been flavored with the leaves of the oregano plant. Flavors such as peppermint and spearmint also come from plant leaves.

Cabbage

Spinach

Lettuce

A. Answer **True** or **False**.

1. The green leaves of vegetables have many vitamins. ___True___

2. Vitamins help the body use carbohydrates and fats. ___True___

B. Answer the questions.

1. What are three kinds of leaves people eat? ___Answers may___ ___vary, but should include: cabbage, spinach,___ ___lettuce, oregano, peppermint, and spearmint.___

2. Where does a cabbage plant store food? ___A cabbage plant___ ___stores food in its leaves.___

Roots

Name these vegetables that have roots that people eat.

A plant's roots take in water and minerals from the soil. Plants use the water and minerals when they make food. Some plants store the food that they make in their roots. For this reason, the roots of some plants are large and thick.

Many of the vegetables that you eat are plant roots. You probably know that carrots are roots. So are beets, turnips, radishes, and parsnips. Carrots are a rich source of vitamin A. This vitamin is needed for the growth of bones and teeth. Vitamin A also keeps the eyes healthy.

Sweet potatoes are also plant roots. These orange potatoes have a sweet taste that many people enjoy. Sweet potatoes have more vitamins than white potatoes. They also have iron and calcium, two minerals that are important for good health. Iron helps the blood carry oxygen. Calcium helps make strong bones and teeth.

Have you ever eaten tapioca pudding? Tapioca comes from the root of one kind of cassava plant. Another kind of cassava plant has roots that are eaten like potatoes. Cassava plants grow in the warm climates of Central and South America.

Many spices and other flavorings come from plant roots. Ginger is a spice that comes from the root of the ginger plant. It is used in ginger ale. It is also used to flavor gingerbread, cookies, and other baked goods. The flavoring for root beer comes from the bark of the sassafras tree root. Sassafras tea is made by boiling the bark.

A. Fill in the missing words.

1. Plants use the water and minerals from the soil when they make ____food____. (leaves, food)

2. Many of the ____vegetables____ that you eat are plant roots. (minerals, vegetables)

3. Two plant roots that people eat are ____carrots and beets____. (carrots and beets, cabbage and spinach)

4. Orange plant roots that have a sweet taste that many people enjoy are ____sweet potatoes____. (white potatoes, sweet potatoes)

5. One kind of ____cassava____ plant has roots that are eaten like potatoes. (tapioca, cassava)

6. A spice that comes from the root of a plant is ____ginger____. (calcium, ginger)

B. Write R after each vegetable that is the root of a plant.

1. carrot ____R____

2. cabbage _____

3. cassava ____R____

4. turnip ____R____

5. lettuce _____

6. beet ____R____

C. Answer True or False.

1. Sweet potatoes have more vitamins than white potatoes. ____True____

2. Carrots are a rich source of vitamin A. ____True____

3. Flavoring for root beer comes from the ginger plant root. ____False____

4. Roots that have food stored in them are large and thick. ____True____

5. Plants use soil when they make food. ____False____

6. Tapioca comes from the bark of the sassafras tree. ____False____

83

Stems

Asparagus

Celery

Rhubarb

Most plants have stems that grow above the ground. Some plants store food in their stems. These stems are thick. They have more starch and sugar in them than the leaves have. They also have minerals and vitamins. People eat the thick stems of many of these plants. For example, the stem of the asparagus plant is eaten as a vegetable. Asparagus is a good source of vitamin A.

Sugar cane is another plant with a thick stem. Sugar cane stems can grow to be 15 feet high. Most of the sugar sold in stores and added to foods comes from the stems of the sugar cane plant.

Celery is a plant stem, or stalk, that has leaves growing from it. People usually eat just the stems and not the leaves. Celery is most often eaten raw, but it can also be cooked. Unlike asparagus, celery has little food value. It is mostly water and salt.

Rhubarb is another plant with a stem that can be eaten. However, the leaves growing from it should never be eaten. Rhubarb leaves have a poison that can make people sick. Rhubarb is not eaten raw. It is cooked and used in pies and other desserts.

Many stems, like celery and rhubarb, are rich in fiber. Fiber is a carbohydrate that cannot be digested. It does, however, help the body digest food.

A. Use the words below to complete the sentences.

asparagus	food	sugar cane
celery	rhubarb	vegetables
fiber	stems	

1. Some plants store food in their _____stems_____ .

2. A plant stem that is a good source of vitamin A is _____asparagus_____ .

3. A plant stem that can grow to be 15 feet high is _____sugar cane_____ .

4. A plant stem that is mostly water and salt is _____celery_____ .

5. Because they have a poison that can make people sick, _____rhubarb_____ leaves should never be eaten.

6. Many stems, like celery, are rich in a carbohydrate called _____fiber_____ .

7. Fiber helps the body digest _____food_____ .

B. Draw lines to complete the sentences.

1. Asparagus   have stems that grow above the ground.
2. Most plants   that store food are thick.
3. Fiber   is used in pies and other desserts.
4. Stems   is a good source of vitamin A.
5. Rhubarb   cannot be digested.

C. Use each word to write a sentence about plant stems.

1. stems _____Sentences will vary._____

   _____

2. fiber _____

   _____

Seeds

Average Percent of Protein Content

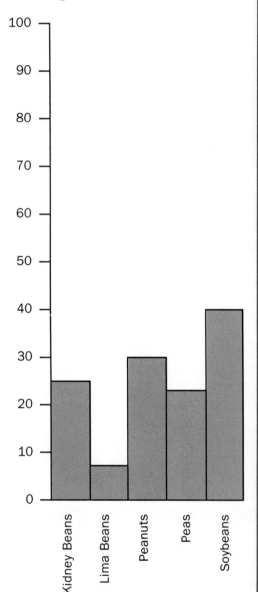

You already know that many plants grow from seeds. Inside a seed is a tiny plant that is partly developed. If a seed is put in the ground and gets enough water, the tiny plant sprouts, or breaks through the seed covering. Until the plant can make its own food, it uses food stored in the seed.

People eat seeds for the food that is stored in them. Peas and beans are seeds that people cook and eat. They are often used to make soup. Peas and beans are a good source of iron, which helps the blood carry oxygen. Most seeds are rich in protein, which the body uses to build and repair cells.

Peanuts are also seeds. They grow underground in pods, or shells. Peanuts are used as food in several ways. They are roasted and eaten. They are ground into peanut butter. They are mixed into candy and baked goods. Peanut oil is widely used in cooking. Peanuts are very healthful to eat. They have a lot of protein and some minerals and vitamins.

Many seeds are eaten as nuts. Some examples are almonds, cashews, chestnuts, hazelnuts, pecans, sunflower seeds, and walnuts. Most nuts are rich in protein.

Soybeans are even richer in protein than nuts. Soybeans are seeds that grow in pods. Soy flour and soy grits are used in cereals, sausages, baked goods, and many other foods. Soy oil is used as cooking oil and in making margarine and salad dressings.

A. Write the letter for the correct answer.

1. People eat seeds for the _____b_____ that is stored in them.
   (a) nuts   (b) food   (c) plants

2. Two kinds of seeds that people cook and eat are peas and _____a_____.
   (a) beans   (b) pods   (c) shells

3. Peanuts grow in _____c_____.
   (a) seeds   (b) nuts   (c) pods

4. Most seeds eaten as nuts are very rich in _____c_____.
   (a) fruits   (b) sugar   (c) protein

5. _____b_____ are even richer in protein than nuts.
   (a) Peanuts   (b) Soybeans   (c) Peas

B. Use the graph on page 86 to answer the questions.

1. Which seeds have the smallest amount of protein? _____lima beans_____

2. Which seeds have the most protein? _____soybeans_____

3. Do peanuts have more or less protein than kidney beans? _____more_____

4. Do peas have more or less protein than lima beans? _____more_____

C. Answer the questions.

1. Until a plant can make its own food, where does it get its food?

   _____Until a plant can make its own food, it uses_____

   _____food stored in the seed._____

2. Why do people eat seeds? _____People eat seeds for the_____

   _____food stored in them._____

3. What does the body use protein to do? _____The body uses_____

   _____protein to build and repair cells._____

4. What are five seeds that people eat? _____Answers may vary,_____

   _____but should include: peas, beans, peanuts, almonds,_____

   _____chestnuts, hazelnuts, pecans, sunflower seeds, walnuts, and soybeans._____

Bulbs and Tubers

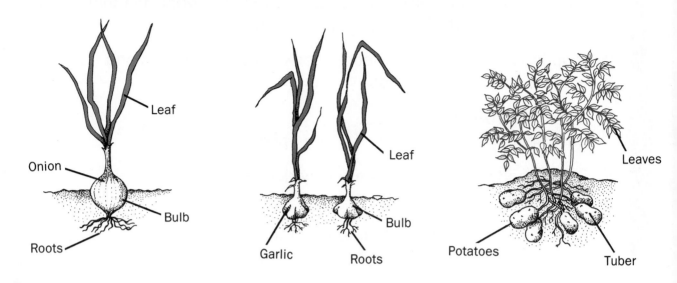

Bulbs and tubers are plant parts that grow under the ground. But they are not roots. Bulbs are thick leaves that grow around a small underground stem. Tubers are thick underground stems.

Onions are the best-known bulbs that people eat. There are many different kinds of onions. Onion bulbs may be purple, white, or yellow. Some have a very strong smell and taste, while others are mild. Onions are usually cooked and used to flavor food, but these vegetables can also be eaten raw. When you cut into a raw onion, a strong oil inside can make your eyes tear.

Garlic is another plant bulb. A garlic bulb is made up of small parts called cloves. Each clove can grow into a new plant. Garlic is usually not eaten as a vegetable. It is mostly used to flavor meats and other foods.

White potatoes are the most commonly eaten plant tubers. Many different kinds of white potatoes are grown throughout the world. They may have brown, pink, or white skins. All potatoes have small buds on their skin called eyes. A new stem can sprout from each eye on a potato. Potatoes are mostly water and starch. But they also have protein, as well as many vitamins and minerals important for a healthy diet.

A. Fill in the missing words.

1. Thick leaves that grow around a small underground stem are _____bulbs_____. (tubers, bulbs)

2. Thick underground stems are _____tubers_____. (tubers, bulbs)

3. The best-known bulbs that people eat are _____onions_____. (onions, potatoes)

4. Garlic is mostly _____used to flavor meats and other foods_____. (eaten as a vegetable, used to flavor meats and other foods)

5. The most commonly eaten plant tubers are _____white potatoes_____. (white potatoes, garlic)

6. Onions are usually cooked and used to flavor food, but they can also be eaten _____raw_____. (raw, in breakfast cereal)

B. Answer True or False.

1. A strong oil inside an onion can make your eyes tear. _____True_____

2. A new stem can sprout from each eye on a potato. _____True_____

3. Bulbs and tubers are plant parts that grow above the ground. _____False_____

4. Potatoes are mostly water and starch, but they also have protein. _____True_____

5. Each clove of a garlic bulb can grow into a new plant. _____True_____

6. Bulbs and tubers are roots. _____False_____

7. Onion bulbs may be purple, white, or blue. _____False_____

C. Use each word to write a sentence about bulbs and tubers.

1. bulbs _____Sentences will vary._____

2. tubers _____

89

Flowers

Broccoli

Cauliflower

When you think of flowers, you may picture tulips or roses. Many flowers are nice to look at. Did you know there are some flowers that people use as food?

One flower you may have eaten is broccoli. Broccoli plants have thick stems. At the tops of the stems are clusters of small green flower buds. If you have eaten broccoli, you have eaten both flowers and stems. Broccoli has large amounts of both vitamins A and C. As you know, vitamin A helps bones and teeth to grow and keeps the eyes healthy. Vitamin C helps the body fight germs.

You may also have eaten cauliflower. Cauliflower is a kind of cabbage and is also related to broccoli. Cauliflower has tightly bunched white flowers that never bloom fully. Like broccoli, cauliflower can be eaten raw or cooked. Cauliflower is a good source of vitamin C.

Even flowers from full-size trees may be part of your diet. When clove trees start to bloom, they have red flower buds. The buds that are picked and dried are called cloves. Cloves are used as a spice. They can be used whole or ground. You may have tasted the spicy flavor of cloves in foods like ham and some cookies.

Although people use only a few kinds of flowers as food, flowers are important in other ways. Flowers form seeds that people can use for food. Some flowers make nectar that bees collect. The bees turn the nectar into honey that people eat. Flowers also form fruits, which you will read about next.

A. Use the words below to complete the sentences.

broccoli	flowers	minerals
cauliflower	food	vitamins
cloves	honey	

1. There are some flowers that people use as _____food_____.

2. If you have eaten _____broccoli_____, you have eaten flowers and stems.

3. Broccoli has large amounts of _____vitamins_____.

4. A kind of cabbage that is also related to broccoli is _____cauliflower_____.

5. Dried flower buds that are used as a spice are _____cloves_____.

6. Although people use only a few kinds as food, _____flowers_____ are important in other ways.

7. Bees turn nectar from flowers into _____honey_____ that people eat.

B. Answer True or False.

1. Cauliflower is a good source of vitamin C. ____True____

2. The vitamin that helps bones and teeth to grow and keeps the eyes healthy is vitamin A. ____True____

3. Flowers and flower buds are not used as food by people. ____False____

4. Cauliflower has tightly bunched white flowers that never bloom fully. ____True____

C. Use each word to write a sentence about flowers used as food.

1. flowers _____Sentences will vary._____

_____

2. food _____

_____

Fruits

Different fruits are good for your diet.

Remember that seeds and fruits are formed by flowers. When egg cells in the ovary of a flower are fertilized, the cells form seeds. The ovary becomes a fruit. Fruits, then, are the parts of a plant that hold the seeds. What do you think tomatoes and cucumbers are? Tomatoes and cucumbers are fruits.

What other fruits do you use as food? You probably eat apples, bananas, strawberries, and blueberries. They are fruits. You may also eat oranges and drink orange juice. All these fruits are very good for your diet. Although they are not good sources of protein, fruits are good sources of vitamins, especially vitamin C, minerals, and fiber.

Different fruits grow in different places, depending on the climate. You probably have eaten fruits that grow in areas that have warm summers and cold winters. Some of these fruits are apples, blueberries, cherries, grapes, peaches, pears, and plums. Dates, grapefruit, lemons, and oranges grow in areas that are warm all year long. Bananas, mangoes, papayas, and pineapples grow where it is hot all year long.

You read about other kinds of fruits earlier in this book. Remember that the grains of cereal plants, like wheat and rice, are also fruits.

A. Write the letter for the correct answer.

1. Seeds and fruits are formed by ____a____ .
   (a) flowers   (b) leaves   (c) roots

2. Fruits are the parts of a plant that hold the ____b____ .
   (a) stems   (b) seeds   (c) flowers

3. Apples and bananas are ____b____ .
   (a) vegetables   (b) fruits   (c) flowers

4. Fruits are good sources of ____c____ .
   (a) orange juice   (b) protein
   (c) vitamins, minerals, and fiber

5. Different fruits grow in different places, depending on ____b____ .
   (a) their size   (b) the climate   (c) their color

6. The grains of ____b____ plants are also fruits.
   (a) apple   (b) cereal   (c) orange

B. Answer True or False.

1. Grapes, grapefruits, and mangoes are fruits. ____True____

2. Tomatoes and cucumbers are not fruits. ____False____

3. Fruits are good sources of vitamins, especially vitamin C. ____True____

4. Fruits are good sources of protein. ____False____

5. The grains of wheat and rice are also fruits. ____True____

6. Papayas and pineapples grow in areas that have warm summers and cold winters. ____False____

C. Answer the questions.

1. Fruits are very good for your diet. What are they good sources of?
   _____Fruits are good sources of vitamins, especially_____
   _____vitamin C, minerals, and fiber._____

2. Fruits are formed by which parts of a plant? _____Fruits are_____
   _____formed by flowers._____

Growing Vegetables

Would you like to grow your own vegetables? You do not need a lot of space. But you do need good soil, plenty of water, and the right amount of sunlight. You can buy seeds for different kinds of vegetables. Read what is written on the package of seeds. It will tell you what conditions your plants will need.

Growing vegetables takes some work. First, you must dig up and remove weeds from the soil of your garden. Next, you plant the seeds. Then it is important to keep watering the soil. When the plants begin to grow, pull out any weeds that grow near the vegetable plants. You may also need to protect your garden from insects or other pests.

You will feel that all your work was worth it when you eat vegetables from your very own garden.

A. The steps below describe how to grow a vegetable garden. Number the steps in the correct order. The first one is done for you.

_____3_____ Keep watering the soil.

_____2_____ Plant seeds.

_____1_____ Dig up and remove weeds from the soil.

_____5_____ Protect your garden from insects and other pests.

_____4_____ Pull out any weeds that grow near the vegetable plants.

B. Answer <u>True</u> or <u>False</u>.

1. To grow your own vegetables, you need good soil, plenty of water, and the right amount of sunlight. _____True_____

2. You need a lot of space to grow vegetables. _____False_____

Part A

Fill in the missing words.

1. People eat the parts of plants where _____food is_____ stored. (flowers are, food is)

2. Spinach ___leaves___ can be cooked or eaten raw. (roots, leaves)

3. Many of the vegetables that you eat, like carrots, are plant ___roots___. (roots, seeds)

4. Many stems, like celery, are rich in ___fiber___. (protein, fiber)

5. Two kinds of seeds that are a good source of iron and protein are _____peas and beans_____. (peas and beans, asparagus and celery)

6. The most commonly eaten plant tubers are _____white potatoes_____. (white potatoes, onions)

7. If you have eaten ___broccoli___, you have eaten both flowers and stems. (lettuce, broccoli)

8. ___Fruits___ are good sources of vitamins, minerals, and fiber. (Fruits, Flowers)

9. To grow your own vegetables, you need good soil, plenty of ___water___, and the right amount of sunlight. (weeds, water)

Part B

Read each sentence. Write <u>True</u> if the sentence is true. Write <u>False</u> if the sentence is false.

1. Onions are the best-known bulbs that people eat. ___True___

2. White potatoes have more vitamins than sweet potatoes. ___False___

3. The food that plants make is a kind of sugar. ___True___

4. Soybeans are even richer in protein than nuts. ___True___

5. Celery is a rich source of vitamin A. ___False___

6. Fruits are the parts of a plant that hold the seeds. ___True___

Create a Salad Collage

You Need

- butcher paper
- old magazines
- index cards
- glue
- markers
- scissors
- encyclopedia or food guide

1. Use a marker to draw the outline of a large salad bowl on the butcher paper.

2. Look through old magazines and cut out pictures of plant parts that could be added to a salad. Draw and cut out any pictures you cannot find.

3. Use an encyclopedia or food guide to find out the vitamins and minerals in each food. Label each picture with the vitamins and minerals it has.

4. Arrange and glue the pictures inside the bowl to create a salad collage. Make sure the foods in your salad have a variety of vitamins and minerals.

5. On an index card, choose six or more items from the collage that you would put in your favorite salad. Create a recipe below your list of ingredients. Collect the recipes to make a class salad cookbook.

Ana's Fruit Salad

blueberries	grapes
strawberries	watermelon
peaches	honeydew melon

Wash all fruit. Slice strawberries and peaches. Cut melon into pieces. Add grapes and blueberries. Chill for one hour.

Write the Answer

Compare the vitamins and minerals in your favorite salad to another salad.

Answers will vary.

Students should compare the vitamins

and minerals in the items in two salads of their choice.

Fill in the circle in front of the word or phrase that best completes each sentence. The first one is done for you.

1. One green leafy vegetable is
   ⓐ beans.
   ⓑ broccoli.
   ● cabbage.

2. The parts of a plant that hold the seeds are the
   ⓐ fruits.
   ⓑ stems.
   ⓒ leaves.

3. Sweet potatoes are plant
   ⓐ bulbs.
   ⓑ roots.
   ⓒ stems.

4. Onions and garlic are plant
   ⓐ bulbs.
   ⓑ stems.
   ⓒ roots.

5. Seeds that have a good supply of protein are
   ⓐ garlic.
   ⓑ grapes.
   ⓒ peanuts.

6. White potatoes are commonly eaten
   ⓐ stems.
   ⓑ tubers.
   ⓒ seeds.

Fill in the missing words.

7. A plant stem that people eat is _____asparagus_____. (asparagus, carrots)

8. Most nuts are rich in _____protein_____. (protein, vitamin C)

9. Soybeans are rich in _____protein_____. (sugar, protein)

Write the answer on the lines.

10. Which parts of a plant are formed by flowers?

   Seeds and fruits are formed by flowers.

UNIT 6
Plant Adaptations

Ocotillo

Small Leaves of Ocotillo

Ocotillo Branch Without Leaves

How Adaptations Help Plants

If you visit different parts of the United States, you will see different **environments.** Environments are the places where plants and animals live. There are hot, dry environments, like the deserts of the Southwest. There are cool, moist environments in the Northeast. Hawaii has a tropical environment where it is warm and wet most of the time. Each environment has a different climate. Different plants grow in each of these environments.

Plants have **adaptations** that help them live in their environment. An adaptation may be a special way that the plant lives. It could also be a special part of a plant. How do adaptations help a plant?

In hot, dry deserts, plants need special adaptations for getting water and holding it. Some cactus plants have deep roots that take up the water from far below the surface of the ground. Other desert plants have roots that spread out near the surface. These roots take in water when it rains. Then the water is stored in the stem of the plant.

Plants lose water through their leaves. Some desert plants have spines in place of leaves. Others, like the ocotillo, have very small leaves. When there is no rain, the leaves of the ocotillo fall off. Then the plant does not lose as much water. When the rain comes, new leaves grow.

Plants have many interesting adaptations. You will read about some of them in this unit.

A. Answer True or False.

1. All environments have the same climate. _____False_____

2. Different plants grow in different environments. _____True_____

3. Plants have adaptations that help them live in their environment.
   _____True_____

4. Plants lose water through their leaves. _____True_____

B. Use the words below to complete the sentences.

deserts	roots	stem
rains	spread out	

In hot, dry _____deserts_____ , plants need special adaptations
for getting water and holding it. Some cactus plants have

_____roots_____ that grow deep into the soil. Other desert plants

have roots that _____spread out_____ near the surface. These roots take

in water when it _____rains_____ . Then the water is stored in the

_____stem_____ of the plant.

C. Answer the questions.

1. What are environments? _____Environments are the places_____
   _____where plants and animals live._____

2. What is an adaptation? _____An adaptation may be_____
   _____a special way a plant lives. It could also_____
   _____be a special part of a plant._____

3. How does an ocotillo save water? _____When there is no rain, the_____
   _____leaves of the ocotillo fall off. Then the plant does not_____
   _____lose as much water. When the rain comes, new leaves grow._____

Parasitic Plants

Dodder

Mistletoe

Some plants do not make enough food for themselves. But they have an adaptation that helps them stay alive. These plants live on other plants and take food from them. A plant that takes food from other plants is called a **parasitic plant.** The plant that a parasitic plant lives on is called a **host.** Parasitic plants can harm a host. Some can even kill their host.

Dodder is a parasitic plant. It has flowers but it does not have leaves. It cannot make its own food. It gets all its food from its host.

The dodder plant has orange, yellow, or brown stems that wrap around a host plant. These tiny threadlike stems grow into the host and take in food made by the host. The dodder plant uses this food to live and grow.

Dodder harms crops like alfalfa and clover. Because of its thin, winding stem, dodder is sometimes called the devil's sewing thread.

Mistletoe is another parasitic plant. It lives mainly on the branches of apple trees. But it may be found on fir trees, sycamores, oaks, and other trees as well. Mistletoe has green oval-shaped leaves that make food for the plant. But mistletoe must get water and minerals from the tree it lives on. Mistletoe often harms its host.

Mistletoe has small yellow flowers and shiny white berries that are poisonous to people. Mistletoe is sometimes used as a decoration at Christmas time.

A. Answer True or False.

1. Some plants do not make enough food for themselves. _____True_____

2. A parasitic plant takes food from other plants. _____True_____

3. The plant that a parasitic plant lives on is called a host. _____True_____

4. Parasitic plants never harm a host. _____False_____

B. Write dodder or mistletoe for each description.

1. has flowers but no leaves _____dodder_____

2. lives on the branches of trees _____mistletoe_____

3. gets water and minerals from its host _____mistletoe_____

4. gets all its food from its host _____dodder_____

5. winds threadlike stems around the host _____dodder_____

6. has yellow flowers and white berries _____mistletoe_____

C. Answer the questions.

1. Some plants do not make enough food for themselves. What adaptation do these plants have to stay alive? _____They can live on other plants and take food from them._____

2. What is a parasitic plant? _____A parasitic plant takes food from other plants._____

3. What is a host plant? _____A host plant is the plant that a parasitic plant lives on._____

4. How does a dodder plant get food from its host? _____It has stems that wrap around a host plant. Threadlike stems grow into the host and take in food made by the host._____

Plants That Attract Insects

The foxglove flowers have marks that guide insects inside the flower.

Roses have sweet smells.

Most plants reproduce from seeds. Seeds are made in flowers. Before seeds can form, a flower must be pollinated. In many plants, insects help pollination take place. These plants have adaptations that attract insects.

Some flowers have marks on their petals. These marks guide an insect inside the flower. The insect gets nectar from inside the flower and uses the nectar for food. The flower, in turn, gets pollinated as the insect moves around inside the flower.

The colors and smells of flowers attract insects, too. Blue, purple, and yellow flowers attract honeybees. Bees and other insects are also attracted to sweet-smelling flowers like roses and honeysuckle. Some flowers bloom at night. These flowers are often white and have a sweet, spicy smell. Moths that fly at night pollinate these flowers.

The shape of a flower is another adaptation that helps pollination take place. Some flowers have large petals that act like landing platforms for bees. The pistil, or female part of the flower, may be just above the platform. As a bee lands, it touches the pistil. Any pollen on the bee gets on the pistil. Then the flower is pollinated.

In tropical areas, some orchids have flowers shaped like female wasps. A male wasp is attracted to the flower and tries to mate with it. The wasp gets pollen on its body. It carries the pollen to the next orchid it visits.

A. Answer True or False.

1. Seeds are made in flowers. __True__

2. Before seeds can form, a flower must be pollinated. __True__

3. Insects help pollination take place in many plants. __True__

4. Plants do not have any adaptations to attract insects. __False__

5. Insects get nectar from inside flowers. __True__

6. Moths pollinate flowers that bloom at night. __True__

B. Fill in the missing words.

1. Blue, purple, and yellow flowers attract __honeybees__. (honeybees, moths)

2. Bees and other insects are attracted to __sweet-smelling__ flowers like roses and honeysuckle. (bad-smelling, sweet-smelling)

3. In tropical areas, some orchids are shaped like female __wasps__. (flowers, wasps)

4. Many plants have adaptations that attract __insects__. (insects, water)

5. An insect gets __nectar__ inside a flower. (water, nectar)

C. Answer the questions.

1. Some flowers have marks on their petals. How do these marks help a flower get pollinated? __The marks guide an insect inside the flower. The flower gets pollinated as the insect moves around inside the flower.__

2. What is one adaptation that plants have to attract insects? __Answers will vary, but should include: marks on their petals, colors, smells, and shapes.__

103

Poisonous Plants

Poison Ivy

Poison Oak

Poison Sumac

For some plants, being poisonous is a special adaptation. Because of this poison, people and animals learn to stay away from these plants.

There are two kinds of poisonous plants. One kind has an effect on the skin of people who touch the plant. The other kind is harmful to people or animals if they eat the plant.

If you touch poison ivy, an oil from the plant can give you an itchy rash. Poison ivy grows in woods and fields. It can form a vine that wraps around trees or other plants. Poison ivy has shiny green leaves in groups of three. The plant also has small green flowers and berries. Poison oak and poison sumac are other plants that give people itchy rashes. It is important to learn what these plants look like so you can avoid them. If you do touch them, wash your skin with soap and water right away.

Fungi are not plants, but you should know that some are harmful if they are eaten. Some mushrooms that grow wild are poisonous. Never eat a mushroom that you find growing. Even tasting a small piece of a poisonous mushroom can be dangerous.

Many garden plants are poisonous if eaten. The flowers of the lily-of-the-valley plant are poisonous. So are daffodils. All parts of azalea plants are poisonous.

Even some parts of food plants are poisonous. You can eat the stems of the rhubarb plant. But there is poison in the leaves. Eating rhubarb leaves can make you sick.

A. Fill in the missing words.

1. People and animals learn to stay away from ____poisonous____ plants. (poisonous, garden)

2. Some plants can give you an itchy rash when you ____touch____ them. (touch, eat)

3. Some mushrooms that grow wild are poisonous to ____eat____. (touch, eat)

4. The parts of the rhubarb plants that are poisonous are the ____leaves____. (stems, leaves)

B. Answer True or False.

1. People will get an itchy rash if they touch an azalea plant.
____False____

2. It is safe to taste a small piece of a poisonous mushroom.
____False____

3. If you touch poison ivy, you should wash your skin with soap and water right away. ____True____

4. For some plants, being poisonous is an adaptation. ____True____

C. Answer the questions.

1. How does being poisonous help a plant? ____People and animals____ ____learn to stay away from the plant.____

2. What is a poisonous plant that is dangerous to eat? ____Answers____ ____may vary but should include: lily-of-the-valley flowers,____ ____daffodil flowers, azalea plants, and rhubarb leaves.____

3. What is a poisonous plant that produces a rash on the skin? ____ ____Answers may vary, but should include: poison ivy,____ ____poison oak, and poison sumac.____

Plants with Spines

Barrel Cactus

Saguaro Cactus

Plants have special adaptations that help them live in their environment. Cactus plants live in desert environments. In a hot, dry desert, only about 10 inches of rain may fall in a year. To live in a desert, a cactus needs special adaptations that help it store water and survive.

Plants lose water through their leaves. In place of leaves, cactus plants have spines. Spines do not lose as much water as broad, flat leaves do. So having spines helps a cactus save water. The sharp spines also help protect a cactus from being eaten by desert animals.

How does a cactus plant make food without leaves? Most of a cactus plant is a stem. The stem has chlorophyll, which makes food for the plant. Both food and water are stored in the stem of a cactus.

There are many kinds of cactus plants. Some are small and low to the ground. Others are bushes. The saguaro cactus can grow to be 50 feet tall. After a rainfall, a saguaro takes in water through its roots. It stores the water in its stem and branches. A large saguaro can hold hundreds of gallons of water.

A. Answer <u>True</u> or <u>False</u>.

1. Cactus plants have broad, flat leaves. ___False___

2. Cactus plants live in cold environments. ___False___

3. Spines help protect a cactus from being eaten by desert animals.

    ___True___

4. Plants lose water through their leaves. ___True___

5. All cactus plants are small and low to the ground. ___False___

6. Both food and water are stored in the stem of a cactus. ___True___

7. In a hot, dry desert, only about 10 inches of rain may fall in a

    year. ___True___

B. Fill in the missing words.

1. Cactus plants grow in ___desert___ environments. (desert, rainy)

2. In place of leaves, cactus plants have ___spines___. (cones, spines)

3. The saguaro stores ___water___ in its stem. (water, leaves)

4. Spines do not lose as much ___water___ as leaves do. (food, water)

5. Plants have special ___adaptations___ that help them live in their
    environment. (adaptations, colors)

C. Use each word to write a sentence about cactus plants.

1. spines _____ Sentences will vary. _____

    _____

2. stem _____

    _____

D. Answer the question.

How do spines help a cactus live in the desert? ___Spines help a___

___cactus save water. They also help protect a cactus___

___from being eaten by desert animals.___

Insect-Eating Plants

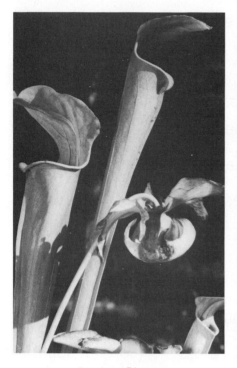

Pitcher Plant

Venus's-Flytrap

A few plants grow in wet places where the soil is poor. Some of these plants can make their own food, but they cannot get all the minerals they need from the soil. So these plants have special adaptations to help them live in their environment. They can trap insects and use them for food. Then the plants get the minerals they need from the insects.

One insect-eating plant is called the pitcher plant. Its leaves are curled into the shape of a pitcher. The pitcher is lined with slippery stiff hairs that point down and in. Insects that are attracted by the plant's fruity smell crawl into the pitcher. But the hairs keep an insect from crawling back out. When an insect falls to the bottom of the pitcher, it drowns in the rainwater that collects there. After a time, the plant digests the insect and takes in the minerals.

There are several kinds of pitcher plants. A common one grows in swampy areas in the eastern part of the United States.

The Venus's-flytrap is another insect-eating plant. It has hinged leaves that are covered with tiny hairs. When an insect lands on a leaf, it touches these hairs. This causes the leaf to close like a trap. The insect can't escape. The plant digests the insect and takes in the minerals that it needs.

The Venus's-flytrap grows best in wet places. It is found mainly in North and South Carolina.

A. Write pitcher plant, Venus's-flytrap, or both for each description.

1. has hinged leaves _____Venus's-flytrap_____

2. grows in wet places _____both_____

3. has a fruity smell _____pitcher plant_____

4. rainwater collects at the bottom of the leaves _____pitcher plant_____

5. uses insects for food _____both_____

6. the leaves close like a trap _____Venus's-flytrap_____

B. Below are the steps that describe how an insect gets trapped in a pitcher plant. Number the steps in the correct order. The first one is done for you.

___2___ The insect crawls into the pitcher.

___1___ An insect is attracted to the pitcher plant.

___5___ The plant digests the insect.

___3___ Hairs inside the pitcher keep the insect from crawling out.

___4___ The insect drowns in rainwater.

C. Answer True or False.

1. Insect-eating plants cannot make their own food. ___False___

2. Insect-eating plants get the minerals they need from insects.

   ___True___

3. Insect-eating plants grow in dry places where the soil is rich.

   ___False___

D. Answer the question.

Why do some plants trap insects? _____They grow in wet places_____
_____where the soil is poor. They cannot get all the minerals_____
_____they need from the soil. The plants get the minerals they_____
_____need from the insects they trap._____

109

The Ant and the Acacia Tree

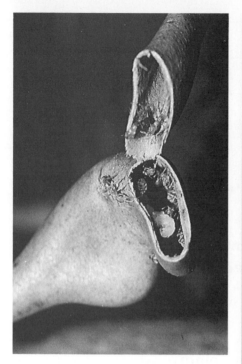

Ants and an Acacia Tree

Plants can be harmed by certain insects. But some insects can actually help plants. This happens with ants and the acacia tree.

The bull's-horn acacia grows in Mexico and Central America. Ants make nests in the large thorns of the tree. They raise their young inside the thorns. The ants also get nectar and other food from the tree.

How do the ants help the tree? Some of the ants act as guards. They attack any insects that try to eat the leaves of the tree. They will even sting cows or other large animals that touch the tree. If any other plants start to grow near the acacia, the ants chew them down.

The ants get a home and food from the tree. The tree is helped, too. It is protected from insects and other animals. It can grow faster than other trees in the area. It does not have to share water, minerals, or sunlight with many other plants.

Answer the questions.

1. What do the ants get from the acacia tree? _____ The ants get _____
   _____ a home and food from the tree. _____

2. How is the acacia tree helped by the ants? _____ Answers may vary, _____
   but should include: The tree is protected from insects and
   other animals. It can grow faster than other trees. It does
   not have to share water, minerals, or sunlight with many
   other plants.

Part A

Read each sentence. Write <u>True</u> if the sentence is true. Write <u>False</u> if the sentence is false.

1. Plants have adaptations that help them live in their environment.

   _____True_____

2. An adaptation can be a special part of a plant. _____True_____

3. A parasitic plant is helpful to other plants. _____False_____

4. Some plants have adaptations that attract insects. _____True_____

5. Some plants are poisonous if they are eaten. _____True_____

6. Plants lose water through their roots. _____False_____

7. In place of leaves, cactus plants have spines. _____True_____

8. Plants never use insects for food. _____False_____

Part B

Use the words below to complete the sentences.

acacia	insects	pollinate
host	poisonous	spines

1. The plant that a parasitic plant lives on is called a _____host_____.

2. In many plants, insects help _____pollinate_____ the flowers.

3. People and animals learn to stay away from _____poisonous_____ plants.

4. Broad, flat leaves lose more water than _____spines_____.

5. Some plants that cannot get enough minerals from the soil can trap

   _____insects_____ for food.

6. An animal and a plant that help each other are ants and the

   _____acacia_____ tree.

Find Plant Adaptations

You Need

- dandelion plant
- local plant
- plant guide books
- drawing paper

1. A dandelion has many adaptations for survival. Its leaves grow flat against the ground. This blocks the sunlight for other plants, so it gets a great deal.

2. A dandelion's flowers turn into a puffball with hundreds of seeds that will grow into new dandelion plants. If you can find a puffball, count the number of seeds it has.

3. Try to dig up the root of a dandelion. This long root stores the plant's winter food supply. New plants will grow from any piece of root left in the ground.

4. Find other nearby plants to study. Try to identify them. Make a labeled drawing of each, and describe the plant's adaptation.

5. Put all the pages together to make a book of plant adaptations.

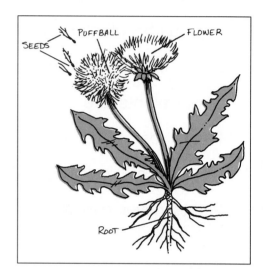

Write the Answer

Which plant would be better adapted to grow in your area—a cactus plant or a rose bush? Explain your answer.

Answers will vary. Students living in hot, dry climates

should choose the cactus. Some students will choose the rose

bush because they have seen one growing nearby.

Fill in the circle in front of the word or phrase that best completes each sentence. The first one is done for you.

1. Places where plants and animals live are called
   ● environments.
   ⓑ adaptations.
   ⓒ deserts.

2. Cactus plants live in
   ⓐ cold places.
   🅑 deserts.
   ⓒ swampy places.

3. Insects help some flowers
   ⓐ grow.
   🅑 get pollinated.
   ⓒ change color.

4. The spines of a cactus
   ⓐ make food.
   ⓑ make water.
   ⓒ help protect the plant and save water.

5. Spines are an adaptation of
   ⓐ cactus plants.
   ⓑ poison ivy.
   ⓒ mushrooms.

6. Insects are attracted to
   ⓐ tall plants.
   ⓑ green leaves.
   ⓒ colorful flowers.

Fill in the missing words.

7. A plant that is poisonous to touch is _____poison ivy_____.
   (poison ivy, dodder)

8. Insect-eating plants grow in _____poor_____ soil.
   (poor, rich)

9. A parasitic plant takes food from _____another plant_____.
   (the soil, another plant)

Write the answer on the lines.

10. How do plants lose water?

    _____Plants lose water through their leaves._____

    _____

    _____

UNIT 7
Plant Products

Wood

Many of the products and materials people use come from plants. One of the most important of these materials is wood. Wood is the part of a tree that forms under the bark. It is made of the tubes that carry water and minerals from the roots to the leaves. Wood must be cut and then dried before it is used.

Wood is a strong material, yet it is light enough to float. Wood doesn't rust. It can help to keep out heat and cold. Because of its properties, wood has many uses. People burn wood to get heat and light. They use wood to build boats. Homes and furniture are made of wood. So are certain kinds of musical instruments. Wood is also important in the making of paper, cloth, and even some kinds of plastics.

Two kinds of wood are used today. One kind, called softwood, comes from conifers. Some common softwoods are fir, pine, and redwood. Softwood is called soft because it is easily cut and shaped by metal tools. But softwood is strong enough to hold heavy weights without breaking. So it is used to build homes. It is also used to make paper and cellophane.

The second kind of wood is hardwood. Hardwood comes from deciduous trees. Some common hardwoods are maple, oak, cherry, and mahogany. Hardwoods have beautiful grains, or patterns. So they are used to make furniture, floors, and decorative objects.

Wood is used to build homes.

This chair is made of wood.

A. Answer True or False.

1. Wood is the part of a tree that forms under the bark. _____True_____

2. Wood is too heavy to float. _____False_____

3. Homes and furniture are made of wood. _____True_____

4. Softwood is too soft to be useful. _____False_____

B. Fill in the missing words.

1. Wood is a strong material, yet it is light enough to _____float_____.
   (float, sink)

2. Wood is important in the making of paper, cloth, and even some

   _____plastics_____. (plastics, food)

3. People burn wood to get heat and _____light_____. (ice, light)

4. Wood is the part of a tree that forms under the _____bark_____.
   (leaves, bark)

5. Two kinds of wood used today are softwood and _____hardwood_____.
   (hardwood, plastic)

6. One common softwood is _____pine_____. (maple, pine)

C. Answer the questions.

1. What kind of trees does softwood come from? _____Softwood comes_____

   _____from conifers._____

2. What is softwood used for? _____Softwood is used to build_____

   _____homes. It is also used to make paper and_____

   _____cellophane._____

3. What kind of trees does hardwood come from? _____Hardwood_____

   _____comes from deciduous trees._____

4. What are hardwoods used for? _____Hardwoods are used to_____

   _____make furniture, floors, and decorative_____

   _____objects._____

Paper

Newspaper

Book

Paper Towels

Milk Carton

What would we do without paper? We write and draw on paper. We read books, magazines, and newspapers printed on paper. We wrap presents and decorate walls with paper. Schools, businesses, and the government use huge amounts of paper every day.

Most paper is made from wood. Wood has properties that help produce good paper. Wood fibers are very strong and hold together well. Wood fibers can also be treated to be stronger, to hold more liquid, and to be fireproof.

Both softwoods and hardwoods are used to make paper. At a paper mill, the bark is removed from logs. Then the logs are cut into tiny pieces. The pieces are cooked until they form a thick pulp.

The wood pulp is then washed and sprayed onto a screen. As water drains off the screen, a thin layer of wood pulp is left. This layer is pressed between rollers to make sheets. Next, the sheets are dried and pressed by hot irons. Then the sheets are cut up into different sizes.

Wood pulp is used to make a thin, clear material called cellophane. Meat and other foods are often wrapped in cellophane packages. Cellophane is waterproof and keeps air away from food. When it is heated, cellophane sticks to itself and makes a tight seal. Cellophane wrappings help keep many foods fresh.

Paper is also made from other plant materials. The best-quality paper is made from cotton rags. Tissues and paper towels may also be made from cotton rags.

A. Answer True or False.

1. Most paper is made from oil. _____False_____

2. The best-quality paper is made from cotton rags. _____True_____

3. Wood fibers are very weak. _____False_____

B. The steps for making paper are listed below. Number the steps in the correct order. The first one is done for you.

___4___ Water drains off the screen, leaving a thin layer of pulp.

___5___ The layer is pressed between rollers to form sheets.

___3___ Pulp is sprayed onto a screen.

___2___ The pieces are cooked until they form a thick pulp.

___1___ Bark is removed from the logs, and the logs are cut into pieces.

___6___ The sheets are dried and pressed by hot irons.

C. Write the letter for the correct answer.

1. Most paper is made from ___a___ .
   (a) wood   (b) rice   (c) corn

2. Paper towels may be made from ___b___ .
   (a) cellophane   (b) cotton rags   (c) oil

3. Wood pulp can be used to make ___c___ .
   (a) trees   (b) oil   (c) cellophane

D. Answer the questions.

1. What kinds of wood are used to make paper? _____Both softwoods_____
   _____and hardwoods are used to make paper._____

2. What are two ways that people use paper? _____Answers may_____
   _____vary, but could include: to write or draw on,_____
   _____to print books, to wrap presents, to decorate_____
   _____walls, and to package foods._____

Medicines

Willow Tree

Purple Foxglove Plant

Most medicines today are made from chemicals in laboratories. But many of these medicines came from plants. For hundreds of years, people have used certain plants as medicines. Plants contain chemicals that affect the human body. Some of these chemicals can kill germs that cause disease. Others can speed up or slow down activities of the body.

People once used the bark of the willow tree to relieve pain and fever. In the 1800s, this drug was finally made in the laboratory. Today, this medicine, called aspirin, is the most common medicine in the world.

A drug called quinine was used for many years to treat a disease called malaria. The drug came from the bark of a tree that grew in the forests of South America. Quinine controls fever, but it does not cure malaria. Today, there are stronger, safer drugs used to treat malaria.

Digitalis is another useful medicine that comes from a plant. It is made from the leaves of the purple foxglove plant. Digitalis is used to make a person's heart beat more regularly.

Scientists study plants throughout the world. They hope that many diseases can be cured by the chemicals found in plants.

A. Answer True or False.

1. For hundreds of years, people have used certain plants as medicines. <u>True</u>

2. Plants contain chemicals that can affect the human body. <u>True</u>

3. Quinine came from the leaves of a tree. <u>False</u>

4. Quinine can cure malaria. <u>False</u>

5. Digitalis is used to make a person's heart beat more regularly.
<u>True</u>

6. Today, aspirin is made in the laboratory. <u>True</u>

7. The most common medicine in the world today is quinine. <u>False</u>

8. Scientists no longer study plants to find cures for diseases.
<u>False</u>

B. Draw lines to match the drug with the plant it comes from.

1. quinine   purple foxglove leaves

2. digitalis   willow bark

3. aspirin   bark of a tree

C. Answer the questions.

1. What are two ways that plant chemicals affect the human body? __
   <u>Some of the chemicals can kill germs that cause</u>
   <u>disease. Others can speed up or slow down</u>
   <u>activities of the body.</u>

2. What was quinine once made from? <u>Quinine came from the</u>
   <u>bark of a tree that grew in the forests of South America.</u>

3. What is digitalis made from? <u>Digitalis is made from the</u>
   <u>leaves of the purple foxglove plant.</u>

119

Cloth

Cotton Plant

Flax Plant

The label inside a shirt tells what material the shirt is made of. Materials such as cotton and linen are natural plant products.

Cotton is the natural fiber used most in the United States. Cotton plants grow in warm, moist climates in the United States and many other countries. Cotton fibers form inside a boll, or pod, after the flowers of the plant die. The boll takes about two months to mature. Then it bursts open. The white cotton fibers are tangled with seeds. To make cotton cloth, the seeds must first be removed from the fibers. Then the fibers are spun into thread. Finally, the thread is woven into cloth.

Linen is a natural fiber made from the flax plant. Flax grows in cool climates where summers are rainy. The flax fibers grow under the woody part of the plant stem. To make linen from flax, the fibers are separated from the stems. Then they are spun into linen thread. Linen is often used to make tablecloths and napkins.

Rayon is another material made from plant parts. It can be made from wood or from cotton. Wood pulp or short cotton fibers are treated with chemicals to make a thick liquid. This liquid is made into rayon threads that are woven into cloth.

A. Fill in the missing words.

1. Materials such as cotton and linen are _____natural_____ . (artificial, natural)

2. ___Cotton___ is the natural fiber used most in the United States. (Cotton, flax)

3. Linen is a natural fiber made from the ___flax___ plant. (cotton, flax)

4. Flax grows in cool climates where summers are ___rainy___ . (rainy, hot)

5. Wood pulp or short cotton fibers can be treated with chemicals to make ___rayon___ . (linen, rayon)

B. Answer True or False.

1. Materials such as cotton and linen are plant products. ___True___

2. Cotton grows in cold climates. ___False___

3. Cotton fibers form inside a boll after the flowers of the plant die. ___True___

4. Flax fibers grow under the woody part of the plant stem. ___True___

5. Rayon is made from flax stems. ___False___

6. Flax grows in cool climates where summers are rainy. ___True___

7. Linen is made from wood pulp or short cotton fibers. ___False___

C. The steps below describe how cotton is made. Number the steps in the correct order. The first one is done for you.

___4___ Then the fibers are spun into thread.

___3___ The seeds are removed from the fibers.

___1___ Cotton fibers form inside a boll.

___5___ The thread is woven into cloth.

___2___ The boll matures and bursts open.

Rubber

Getting Latex From a Rubber Tree

The tires on a bicycle or a car are made of natural rubber. Natural rubber is a plant product. It comes from rubber trees that grow in hot, moist climates.

Natural rubber is made from a milky liquid called **latex.** When slits are made in the bark of a rubber tree, latex oozes out. Then the liquid can be collected. A rubber tree can produce latex for up to 30 years.

Rubber has many properties that make it a very useful material. Rubber is elastic. An elastic material can stretch and go back to its original shape. It can bounce and absorb shocks. Rubber tires can roll over holes and bumps in a road without being damaged. Because rubber lasts a long time, rubber products do not wear out quickly. Because rubber is waterproof, it is used to make boots, raincoats, gloves, and hats.

Finally, rubber does not let electricity pass through it. So it is used to cover, or insulate, wires that carry electricity. This protects people from electric shock and prevents fires.

Answer True or False.

1. Natural rubber comes from a tree. ___True___

2. Rubber is not an elastic material. ___False___

3. Rubber trees grow in hot, moist climates. ___True___

4. Rubber lets electricity pass through it. ___False___

5. Rubber is made from a milky liquid called latex. ___True___

122

Part A

Use the words below to complete the sentences.

aspirin	cotton	latex	quinine
cellophane	elastic	medicines	Rayon
conifers	homes	oak	wood

1. Today, wood is mostly used to build _____homes_____.

2. Most paper is made from _____wood_____.

3. Softwood comes from trees called _____conifers_____.

4. A common kind of hardwood is _____oak_____.

5. Natural rubber is made from a milky liquid called _____latex_____.

6. The natural plant fiber used most in the United States is _____cotton_____.

7. A drug that was used to treat malaria is _____quinine_____.

8. Because rubber is _____elastic_____, it can stretch and go back to its original shape.

9. Wood pulp is used to make a thin, clear material called _____cellophane_____.

10. Most _____medicines_____ today are made from chemicals in laboratories.

11. _____Rayon_____ can be made from wood or from cotton.

Part B

Draw lines to match the plant products with their uses.

1. aspirin —— make cloth

2. cotton —— relieve pain and fever

3. wood —— make heart beat regularly

4. digitalis —— build homes

5. wood pulp —————— make paper

123

Make Your Own Recycled Paper

You Need

- partner
- newspaper
- water
- $\frac{1}{2}$ gallon container
- eggbeater
- 10" x 10" aluminium screen
- 1" x 10" board
- cafeteria tray

1. Tear one full page of newspaper into tiny pieces. Soak the pieces in a container of warm water overnight.

2. Mix with your hands to break up any clumps. Beat with an eggbeater until you have a smooth pulp.

3. Place some newspaper on the tray. Place the screen on top. Scoop the pulp onto the screen and spread it with your hands to make an even layer.

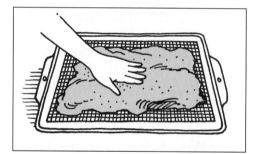

4. Put the board on top of the pulp-covered screen. Put books or other heavy objects on the board to squeeze out excess water. Replace the paper under the screen until the water has been squeezed out.

5. Carefully peel the pulp off the screen. Let it dry for at least one day. When it is dry, you can write on it with a felt marker.

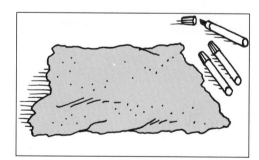

Write the Answer

Explain what you think would happen if you used other kinds of paper.

Many students will correctly infer

that other kinds of paper could be used

in this activity to make paper.

124

Fill in the circle in front of the word or phrase that best completes each sentence. The first one is done for you.

1. Wood is the part of a tree that forms under the
   - ⓐ leaves.
   - ⓑ roots.
   - ● bark.

2. Maple, oak, and cherry are three kinds of
   - ⓐ softwood.
   - ⬤ⓑ hardwood.
   - ⓒ bark.

3. Softwood from conifers is used to
   - ⬤ⓐ build homes.
   - ⓑ make medicine.
   - ⓒ make cloth.

4. A medicine that comes from the purple foxglove plant is
   - ⓐ quinine.
   - ⬤ⓑ digitalis.
   - ⓒ aspirin.

5. The most common medicine in the world is
   - ⬤ⓐ aspirin.
   - ⓑ quinine.
   - ⓒ digitalis.

6. The natural fiber used most in the United States comes from the
   - ⓐ rubber tree.
   - ⬤ⓑ cotton plant.
   - ⓒ oak tree.

Fill in the missing words.

7. Most paper is made from _____wood_____. (cloth, wood)

8. A fiber that is made from the flax plant is _____linen_____. (rubber, linen)

9. Wires that carry electricity are insulated with _____rubber_____. (rubber, paper)

Write the answer on the lines.

10. What are two properties of the plant product called rubber?

   Answers may vary but should include:

   rubber is a plant product that is elastic, is waterproof, lasts a long time,

   and does not let electricity through.

UNIT 8
Conservation

We must protect our natural resources. We could not live without them.

Protecting Plants

Conservation is the protection and wise use of our **natural resources.** Natural resources are things from Earth that people find useful. Water, soil, and minerals are natural resources. Plants are an important natural resource, too, because people and other animals could not live without them.

Most of the foods we eat come from plants or from animals that eat plants. We use wood from trees to build our homes. Most of the paper we use also comes from wood. Even some of the clothes we wear are made from plant fibers. Plants are very important to people.

As the number of people living on Earth grows, more of the land is used to build cities, farms, and roads. This leaves less space for plants and animals to live. As a result, some plants are becoming **endangered.** An endangered plant is one that is so rare it can only be found growing in small numbers. It is in danger of becoming **extinct.** A plant becomes extinct when every one of its kind has died. **Conservationists** are people who work to make sure that our natural resources are not destroyed. They try to identify endangered plants and animals. To protect these living things, they set aside places where these rare plants and animals can live and grow. Conservationists also manage our forests to be sure we have enough wood, clean water, and air. In this unit, you will learn more about the importance of conservation for plant life.

A. Fill in the missing words.

1. Conservation is the protection and wise use of our
   ___natural resources___. (minerals, natural resources)

2. Water, soil, and ___minerals___ are natural resources.
   (plastic, minerals)

3. We use ___wood___ from trees to build our homes. (wood, leaves)

4. An endangered plant is one that is so rare it can only be found
   growing in ___small___ numbers. (large, small)

5. A plant becomes ___extinct___ when every one of its kind has
   died. (safe, extinct)

B. Answer True or False.

1. Plants are not important to people. ___False___

2. Natural resources are things from Earth that people find useful.
   ___True___

3. As the number of people living on Earth grows, there is more
   space for plants and animals to live. ___False___

4. Conservationists are people who work to make sure that our
   natural resources are destroyed. ___False___

5. Most of the foods we eat come from plants or from animals that
   eat plants. ___True___

C. Answer the questions.

1. What is conservation? ___Conservation is the protection and___
   ___wise use of our natural resources.___

2. What are two natural resources that people find useful? ___Answers___
   ___may vary, but should include: water, soil, minerals,___
   ___and plants.___

Endangered Plants

This rare lily can only be found growing on hillsides near San Francisco, California.

You have probably heard more about endangered animals than endangered plants. This is because most endangered plants in the United States are rare and can only be found in certain places. Their numbers may also be very small. For example, there is an endangered lily that grows only on hillsides near San Francisco, California. Unless you live nearby, you might never see or hear about this plant.

Nearly 500,000 kinds of plants have been identified on Earth. There may be 500,000 more unknown kinds, many in tropical rain forests. These plants are in the greatest danger of becoming extinct.

The tropical rain forests are being cut down at a very fast rate. Scientists know very little about the plants in these forests. There may be plants that have not been discovered yet. But the plants may become extinct before we can study them.

Most of the food we grow as crops came from wild plants first found in the tropics. Many medicines were developed from tropical plants. Letting undiscovered plants become extinct is like throwing away a present before unwrapping it.

Destroying the places where plants live is just one way in which plants become endangered. Some plants are not able to survive when the air or water contains harmful chemicals. People often raise cattle, sheep, and horses in dry grassland areas. But if too many animals graze in an area, the plants cannot survive. Ranchers can manage their lands so that plants do not become endangered.

A. **Use the words below to complete the sentences.**

growing	medicines	survive
lily	plants	tropics

1. Most endangered plants in the United States are rare and can only be found ___growing___ in certain places.

2. There is an endangered ___lily___ that grows only on hillsides near San Francisco, California.

3. There are about 235,000 kinds of ___plants___ growing on Earth today.

4. Most of the food we grow as crops came from plants first found in the ___tropics___ .

5. Some plants cannot ___survive___ when the air or water contains harmful chemicals.

6. Many ___medicines___ were developed from tropical plants.

B. **Answer True or False.**

1. Some plants may become extinct before we have a chance to study them. ___True___

2. Scientists know everything about the plants growing in the rain forest. ___False___

3. Two thirds of the plants growing on Earth today are found in the tropical rain forests. ___True___

4. The tropical rain forests are being saved. ___False___

5. If too many animals graze in an area, the plants cannot survive. ___True___

6. Some plants are not able to survive when the air or water contains harmful chemicals. ___True___

129

Forest Conservation

To help protect the forest, new trees must be planted in place of those that are cut down.

Forests are important to people in many ways. We use wood from the forest trees to build our homes. Wood is also used to make furniture, paper, and many other products. Forests must be managed wisely so we can continue to have a supply of wood and a clean water supply.

Three hundred years ago, much of the United States was covered by forests. But settlers cut down many of the trees. They cleared the land for their farms and towns. Slowly people realized that our forests were being destroyed.

Today, many of our forests are protected. Areas of land are set aside as national forests. People can visit national forests and enjoy nature. At the same time, these forests provide a safe home for many plants and animals.

In a national forest, lumber companies are allowed to cut down a certain number of trees each year. But they have to plant new trees in their place. This helps to make sure that we will have trees and wood products in the future.

There is another way that forests are important to people. The soil in a forest soaks up large amounts of water. This helps to prevent flooding. The water soaks into the ground. As the underground water flows through the soil, it is cleaned. It becomes a fresh supply of water for streams, rivers, and lakes.

A. Write the letter for the correct answer.

1. Forests are important to people in ____a____.
   (a) many ways   (b) one way only   (c) no way at all

2. Forests must be managed wisely so that we can continue to have a
   supply of ____b____.
   (a) leaves   (b) wood   (c) dirt

3. Three hundred years ago, much of the United States was covered with
   ____c____.
   (a) ice   (b) water   (c) forests

4. National forests provide a safe home for many ____b____.
   (a) people   (b) plants and animals   (c) rivers

B. Answer True or False.

1. We no longer use wood from forest trees to build homes. __False__

2. In the past, settlers cut down many trees and cleared the land for
   their farms and towns. __True__

3. Today, many of our forests are protected. __True__

4. People cannot visit national forests. __False__

5. In a national forest, lumber companies are allowed to cut down as
   many trees as they want each year. __False__

6. The soil in a forest soaks up large amounts of water. __True__

C. Use each word to write a sentence about our national forests.

1. wood _____Sentences will vary._____
   _____

2. water _____
   _____

131

Forests in Danger

The rain forests may be disappearing at the rate of 1 acre every second.

Tropical rain forests grow where it is hot and wet all year long. These forests make up about half of the forested land on Earth. Large areas of South America and Southeast Asia are covered with rain forests. The Amazon in South America is the largest rain forest in the world. This rain forest is about two-thirds the size of the entire United States!

In recent years, much of the rain forest has been cleared. The trees are being cut down and burned. Houses, farms, and large ranches are taking their place. In the 1990s, more than 1 acre of rain forest was cut down every second! At that rate, much of the world's rain forests would soon have been destroyed.

The soil of a rain forest is not good for farming. In the hot sun, the thin soil dries out and gets hard. Then it is easily washed away by rain. Every few years, farmers clear more forest to find new soil.

What will happen if all the rain forests are destroyed? As the forests are cleared and burned, carbon dioxide is given off. Too much carbon dioxide in the air will make the temperature on Earth warmer. This would cause ice near the North and South Poles to melt. The water level in the oceans would rise. Cities along coastlines would be underwater. People need to find a way to protect the rain forests.

A. Answer True or False.

1. Tropical rain forests grow where it is cold and dry. _____False_____

2. The Amazon in South America is the largest rain forest in the world. _____True_____

3. Today, much of the rain forest is being saved. _____False_____

4. The soil of a rain forest is very good for farming. _____False_____

5. Too much carbon dioxide in the air will make the temperature on Earth warmer. _____True_____

B. Write the letter for the correct answer.

1. Tropical rain forests make up _____b_____ of the forested land on Earth.
   (a) all   (b) about half   (c) a small part

2. In the 1990s, more than 1 acre of rain forest was cleared _____a_____.
   (a) every second   (b) every five days   (c) every year

3. At that rate, much of the world's rain forests would _____b_____.
   (a) be saved   (b) have been destroyed   (c) grow back

4. As the rain forests are cleared and burned, _____c_____ is given off.
   (a) water   (b) oxygen   (c) carbon dioxide

C. Answer the questions.

1. What happens to the soil of the rain forest in the hot sun? _____In the_____
   _____hot sun, the thin soil dries out and gets hard._____
   _____Then it can easily be washed away by rain._____
   _____

2. What will happen if ice near the North and South Poles begins to melt? _____The water level in the oceans would rise._____
   _____Cities along coastlines would be underwater._____

People Can Protect Plants

Recycling helps save resources.

People can be a threat to plants. But we can also help protect plants from becoming extinct. How can we do this?

In the United States, we have laws to protect plants and their environments. We set aside land where endangered plants can grow. Many countries do not have laws to protect plants. We can support programs to protect plants throughout the world.

People can use plant products wisely. We can recycle paper so that fewer trees are cut down.

People must use chemicals carefully. Certain chemicals that get in the air and water can harm plants and animals.

Plants are as important as the air we breathe. We must learn to share our planet with them. Without plants, we would not be able to survive.

Fill in the missing words.

1. People can help to protect plants from becoming ___extinct___.
   (extinct, safe)

2. We can recycle ___paper___ so that fewer trees are cut down.
   (paper, water)

3. Certain ___chemicals___ that get into the air and water can harm plants and animals. (chemicals, plants)

134

Part A

Use the words below to complete the sentences.

chemicals	extinct	rare
	natural resources	

1. Conservation is the protection and wise use of our __natural resources__ .

2. A plant becomes __extinct__ when every one of its kind has died.

3. An endangered plant is one that is so __rare__ it can only be found growing in very small numbers.

4. Some plants are not able to survive when the air or water contains harmful __chemicals__ .

Part B

Read each sentence. Write <u>True</u> if the sentence is true. Write <u>False</u> if the sentence is false.

1. People could not live without plants. __True__

2. Natural resources are things from Earth that people cannot use.
   __False__

3. Two thirds of all plants growing on Earth today are found in the tropical rain forests. __True__

4. If too many animals graze in an area, the plants cannot survive.
   __True__

5. Areas are set aside as national forests so that lumber companies can cut trees down. __False__

Start a Recycling Program

You Need

- large, sturdy boxes
- bundled newspapers
- poster paper
- markers

1. Study the chart to see how much paper is used and thrown away. You can start a recycling program to help save the trees.

2. Newspapers are easy to recycle. Call your local waste management to find out about recycling programs in your area.

3. Set a goal. How many trees do you want to save? You will save 17 trees for each ton of paper you recycle. If you recycled three tons of newspaper, you would save over 50 trees!

4. Get several large boxes in which to collect the newspapers. Put the boxes in a place where they are easy to reach.

5. Make colorful posters inviting others to help your class reach its goal. Display the posters in the office, hallways, and local stores. Have volunteers help to transport the bundled newspapers.

Facts on Paper Waste in the U.S.

- U.S. citizens use 50 million tons of paper each year. That means cutting down a billion trees.
- About 63 million newspapers are printed every day in the U.S.
- If each family recycled the Sunday newspaper, 500,000 trees would be saved each week. That would save 30 million trees each year!
- Every U.S. citizen uses two trees' worth of paper each year.
- Every ton of paper that is recycled saves 17 trees.

Help Our Class Save 50 Trees!

Bring your bundled newspapers to the office.

We Need Your Help!

Write the Answer

Describe how you would plan to recycle aluminum cans.

Answers will vary. Answers may include starting a larger recycling

program where cans are recycled. Steps would be similar to finding

out about recycling papers by calling a local waste management office.

Fill in the circle in front of the word or phrase that best completes each sentence. The first one is done for you.

1. A plant becomes extinct when every one of its kind has
   - ⓐ moved away.
   - ● died.
   - ⓒ started to grow.

2. An endangered plant is so rare it can only be found growing in
   - ⓐ small numbers.
   - ⓑ large numbers.
   - ⓒ cold areas.

3. Conservationists work to make sure our natural resources are
   - ⓐ used up.
   - ⓑ endangered.
   - ⓒ not destroyed.

4. We use wood from forest trees to
   - ⓐ build homes.
   - ⓑ make furniture and paper.
   - ⓒ both a and b.

5. Today, much of the rain forest is being
   - ⓐ cut down and burned.
   - ⓑ planted with new trees.
   - ⓒ blown away by the wind.

6. Two thirds of the plants found growing today are
   - ⓐ not endangered.
   - ⓑ found in tropical rain forests.
   - ⓒ found in cold areas.

Fill in the missing words.

7. Some plants cannot survive when the air or water contains ___harmful chemicals___. (dust, harmful chemicals)

8. To protect plants people should ___use chemicals carefully___. (burn down forests, use chemicals carefully)

9. When trees are cut down, the soil of the rain forest ___dries out in the hot sun___. (is good for farming, dries out in the hot sun)

Write the answer on the lines.

10. Why are certain areas of land set aside as national forests?

    ___Certain areas of land are set aside as national forests___

    ___to help protect the forests.___

137

A   **adaptation,** page 98.
An adaptation may be a special way that a plant lives. It could also be a special part of a plant. Adaptations help plants live in their environment.

algae, page 18.
Algae are plants that do not have tubes. Most algae live in oceans, lakes, and ponds.

annual, page 33.
An annual plant is a plant that lives for just one year. Many wildflowers are annual plants.

B   **bamboo,** page 52.
Bamboo is a giant perennial grass that lives for many years. Bamboo stems are stronger than other grass stems.

bark, page 56.
Bark is the tough outside layer of a tree trunk. Bark protects a tree from insects, disease, and from too much heat or cold.

blades, page 40.
Blades are the spear-shaped leaves of grass plants. Blades grow from jointed stems.

botany, page 4.
Botany is the study of plant life.

bud, page 16.
A bud is a bulge that forms on a yeast cell. The bud grows into a new yeast cell.

bulb, page 31.
A bulb is a kind of underground stem with leaves that store food. Tulip flowers grow from bulbs. Onions are bulbs that people eat.

C   **canopy,** page 64.
The canopy is the layer of a forest formed by the tallest trees. It gets most of the sunlight in the forest.

cap, page 17.
A cap is the top of a mushroom stalk. Spores are made underneath the cap.

carbohydrates, page 80.
Carbohydrates are substances that help the body produce energy. Sugars and starches are carbohydrates.

carbon dioxide, page 6.
Carbon dioxide is a gas from the air. Plants use carbon dioxide in making food.

cells, page 4.
Cells are the tiny parts that plants are made up of. Cells cannot be seen without a microscope.

chlorophyll, page 6.
Chlorophyll is the material that makes leaves green. Chlorophyll helps plants make food.

conifer, page 60.
A conifer is a tree that makes cones. The seeds of conifers are made in the cones. Pine, spruce, fir, and sequoia trees are conifers.

coniferous forest, page 66.
A coniferous forest is a forest that is made up mainly of conifers.

conservation, page 126.
Conservation is the protection and wise use of our natural resources.

conservationist, page 126.
A conservationist is a person who works to make sure that natural resources are not destroyed. A conservationist also tries to identify and protect endangered plants and animals.

corn, page 46.
Corn is an annual cereal grass. It is the most important crop in the United States. Its most important use is as a food for farm animals.

D   **deciduous,** page 62.
A deciduous tree is one that loses all its leaves at a certain time each year. Birch, beech, hickory, oak, and maple are deciduous trees.

deciduous forest, page 64.
A deciduous forest is a forest that is made up mostly of deciduous trees.

E   **endangered,** page 126.
An endangered plant is one that is so rare that it can only be found growing in small numbers.

environment, page 98.
An environment is the place where plants and animals live. There are many different kinds of environments.

evergreen, pages 8, 60.
An evergreen is a tree that does not lose all its leaves in the fall. Many evergreens have leaves shaped like needles.

extinct, page 126.
A plant becomes extinct when every one of its kind has died.

ferns, page 20.
Ferns are plants with tubes. They have leaves, stems, and roots, so they are sometimes called true plants.

fertilize, page 10.
When pollen enters the female cells of a flower, the cells are fertilized. Fertilized female cells make seeds.

fibrous roots, page 56.
Fibrous roots are a system of roots that spread out in the soil. Some trees have fibrous roots.

forest, page 64.
A forest is a place where many trees grow. Many smaller plants and a variety of animals are also found in a forest.

fruit, page 24.
A fruit holds the seeds that form in a flower. A fruit can be soft and fleshy like a peach, or hard like a walnut.

fungi, page 14.
The fungi are a group of living things that can grow and reproduce. But they cannot make their own food. Mushrooms are one kind of fungi.

grains, page 40.
Grains are the fruit of grass plants.

grasses, page 40.
Grasses are plants that have jointed stems and long, spear-shaped leaves. Many cereal grasses, such as wheat, corn, rice, and oats are used for food.

growth ring, page 58.
In a tree, new wood is made of tubes that form in a circle called a growth ring. A new growth ring forms every year.

heartwood, page 56.
Heartwood is the oldest, darkest, and hardest wood of a tree. Heartwood helps support a tree.

host, page 100.
A host is a plant that a parasitic plant lives on. A host can be harmed and even killed by a parasitic plant.

I

inner bark, page 56.
The inner bark is the part of a tree between the sapwood and the bark. Food that is made in the leaves is carried to other parts of the tree through the inner bark.

L

latex, page 122.
Latex is the milky liquid from a rubber tree. Natural rubber is made from latex.

lawn grasses, page 42.
Lawn grasses are short perennial grass plants that are used to cover ball fields, playgrounds, and yards.

leaves, page 6.
The leaves are the parts of a plant where food is made.

M

microscope, page 4.
A microscope is a tool that helps you see very small things.

minerals, page 6.
Minerals are substances that plants need to grow. The water taken in by the roots of a plant carry the needed minerals.

mold, page 15.
A mold is a kind of fungi. Molds cannot make their own food. They get their food from the things they live on.

moss, page 19.
Moss is a very small plant that does not have tubes. Moss has chlorophyll and can make its own food.

mushroom, page 17.
A mushroom is a kind of fungi. It cannot make its own food. Some mushrooms are safe to eat, but others are poisonous.

N

natural resources, page 126.
Natural resources are things from Earth that people find useful. Water, soil, and minerals are natural resources.

nectar, page 26.
Nectar is a sweet liquid that is made inside a flower. Some insects feed on nectar.

O

oats, page 50.
Oats are a kind of annual cereal grass. Most oats are used as food for farm animals.

ovary, page 24.
The ovary is the part of a flower that holds the egg cells. The ovary develops into a fruit.

ovules, page 24.
Ovules are egg cells in the ovary of a flower. Ovules are fertilized by pollen cells. Then they start to form seeds.

oxygen, page 6.
The leaves of plants give off a gas called oxygen into the air. People and other animals take in oxygen when they breathe.

P

parasite, page 14.
A parasite is a living thing that lives on or in living plants or animals. Some fungi are parasites.

parasitic plant, page 100.
A parasitic plant is a plant that lives on other plants and takes food from them. Mistletoe is a parasitic plant.

perennial, page 30.
A perennial plant is a plant that can grow year after year, without being replanted. Some flowers, like daisies and violets, are perennials.

petals, page 24.
Petals are the parts of flowers that are usually colored. The colors help attract insects and other animals to the flowers.

photosynthesis, page 8.
Photosynthesis is the way that plants make food.

pistil, page 24.
The pistil is the female part of a flower.

plants, page 4.
Plants make up one group of living things. Plants can grow, reproduce, and make their own food. Most plants have roots, stems, and leaves.

pollen, pages 10, 24.
Pollen is a powder made by the male parts of a flower. Pollen fertilizes the female cells of a flower.

pollination, page 26.
Pollination is moving pollen from the stamens of a flower to the pistil. The wind, insects, and even bats help pollination take place.

R

reproduce, page 4.
To reproduce means to make more living things. Plants can make new plants just like themselves.

rhizome, page 40.
A rhizome is the underground stem of some perennial grasses. Rhizomes spread out to start new grass plants.

rice, page 48.
Rice is an annual cereal grass. Both brown and white rice can be eaten. Rice is the main food for many people, especially people living in Asia.

root, page 6.
The part of a plant that is in the ground is called the root. Many of the vegetables that people eat are plant roots.

root hairs, page 6.
The tips of roots are covered with tiny root hairs that take in water from the soil.

S

sap, page 56.
Sap is the mixture of water and minerals in the tubes of a tree.

saprophyte, page 14.
A saprophyte is a living thing that lives on the bodies of dead animals. Some fungi are saprophytes.

sapwood, page 56.
Sapwood is the part of a tree that has the tubes that carry water and minerals from the roots to the leaves.

seed, page 10.
A seed is a part of a plant that can grow into a new plant. Many kinds of plants reproduce from seeds.

sepals, page 24.
Sepals are the parts of a flower that protect the flower when it is a bud. Sepals are green and look like leaves.

spore, page 10.
A spore is a special cell that can live a long time without water. Mosses and ferns reproduce from spores.

stalk, page 17.
A stalk is the stemlike part of a mushroom. It grows above the ground.

stamens, page 24.
Stamens are the male parts of flowers. Pollen is made in the top part of the stamens.

stem, page 6.
The stem is the part of a plant that helps hold up the plant. The stem carries water and minerals from the roots up to the leaves.

140

sugar cane, page 51.
Sugar cane is a perennial grass that can grow for many years. Sugar is made from the stems of sugar cane plants.

taproot, page 56.
A taproot is a root that grows straight down in the soil. Some trees have one main taproot.

tropical rain forest, page 68.
A tropical rain forest is a forest that grows where the weather is hot and wet all year round.

trunk, page 56.
A trunk is the hard, woody stem of a tree. It is made up of several layers.

tubes, page 12.
Tubes are the parts of plants that carry water and minerals from the soil to the leaves. They also carry food from the leaves to other parts of the plant.

U understory, page 64.
The understory is the middle layer of a forest. It is formed by the tops of shorter trees.

W weed, page 42.
A weed is a plant that grows where it is not wanted. A dandelion is one kind of weed.

wheat, page 44.
Wheat is an annual cereal grass. Both white flour and whole-wheat flour come from wheat. Many people throughout the world use wheat for food.

wildflower, page 33.
A wildflower is a flower that is not planted by people. Asters are a kind of wildflower.

Y yeast, page 16.
Yeast is part of the fungi group. Like other fungi, it cannot make its own food. Yeast is used to make bread light and fluffy.

Acknowledgments

Illustrations

Accurate Art, Inc.—**10,12**
Kathie Kelleher—**22, 38, 54, 78, 96, 112, 124**
Art Kretzschmar—**28, 29, 40, 44, 46, 116**
Laurie O'Keefe—**56, 70, 71**
Erika Kors—**81, 82, 84, 88, 90, 92**
All Other Illustrations
Don Collins and Lewis Calver

Photographs

P.**4 (bottom)** © Westlight/Mark Stephenson/CORBIS; p.**15** © Clouds Hill Imaging, Ltd./CORBIS; p.**18** © Peter Menzel/Stock Boston; p.**19 (left)** © Doug Sokell/Tom Stack & Associates, **(right)** © Grant Heilman Photography; p.**20 (top)** © Grant Kalivada/Tom Stack & Associates, **(bottom)** Texas Highways; p.**24** © Runk/Schoenberger/Grant Heilman Photography; p.**32** © Grant Heilman Photography; p.**33** © Ken W. Davis/Tom Stack & Associates; p.**34 (bottom)** © Dan Sams/Getty Images; p.**36** © Dick Keen/Unicorn Stock Photos; p.**42 (bottom)** Dwight Kuhn; pp.**48, 50** © Grant Heilman Photography; p.**52** © Dave Miller/Tom Stack & Associates; p.**60** US Forest Service; p.**62** Gerard Fritz/Transparencies; pp.**64, 66** © Grant Heilman Photography; p.**68** Richard E. Ferguson/William E. Ferguson; p.**70** © Grant Heilman Photography; p.**71** © Ralph A. Clevenger/CORBIS; p.**72** © Raymond Gehman/CORBIS; p.**74** US Forest Service; p.**76 (top)** Jane Faircloth/Transparencies, **(bottom)** Texas Highways; p.**80** Bureau of Reclamation, Ephrata, WA; p.**94** © Larry Lefever/Grant Heilman Photography; p.**98 (middle)** © Richard Cummins/CORBIS, **(bottom)** Tonto National Monument; p.**100 (top)** Zoological Society of San Diego, **(bottom)** © Grant Heilman Photography; p.**102 (top)** © Grant Heilman Photography; p.**104 (top)** © Grant Heilman Photography, **(middle)** © Jeri Gleiter/Getty Images, **(bottom)** © John Gerlach/Tom Stack & Associates; p.**106 (left)** Henry E. Huntington Library, **(right)** © John Shaw/Tom Stack & Associates; p.**108 (top)** Texas Highways, **(bottom)** © Tom Stack & Associates; p.**110** © Chip Isenhart/Tom Stack & Associates; p.**114 (top)** © Ann Duncan/Tom Stack & Associates, **(bottom)** Shaker Heritage Society; p.**118 (left)** © Grant Heilman Photography; p.**120** © Grant Heilman Photography; p.**122** © Owen Franken/CORBIS; p.**128** Steve McCormick/The Nature Conservancy; p.**130** © Grant Heilman Photography; p.**132** Rainforest Action Network; p.**134** © David Young-Wolfe/PhotoEdit.

Additional photography by Royalty-Free/CORBIS, PhotoDisc/Getty Royalty Free, Photos.com Royalty Free, and PhotoSpin Royalty Free.